BREAKING FREE

A MOTHER'S PROMISE

SANMAATRIKA

This book is dedicated to my daughter,
My breath in another body,
My silent prayer in every moment.

And to every mother who clings to faith,
even when the world asks her to let go.

Contents

"A mother's love is the quiet force that breaks chains, crosses oceans, and defies destiny because when her child is lost, she becomes the storm that brings her home."

Preface

Dear Reader,

In a world that often celebrates love and resilience, the shadows of manipulation and deception quietly thrive, unseen, underestimated, and deeply destructive.

This book is not just a journal based on the true events from my life, it is also a wake-up call. It is a testament to the unbreakable strength of a mother's love and a solemn reminder of how even the closest bonds can be tested, twisted, and torn by forces that prey on vulnerability in the guise of faith or guidance.

When my journey began, I never imagined the trials that lay ahead or the strength I would be forced to summon. My daughter, my pride, my heartbeat, my closest companion, was drawn into a world I couldn't recognize. A world draped in the veil of spirituality, but built upon control, coercion, and calculated deceit.

She was the little girl who once ran into my arms for comfort, who whispered her dreams to me at night, and whose laughter gave meaning to my days. Watching her drift away, emotionally and physically, was like watching the light of my life slowly dim, while I stood powerless, screaming in silence.

This book is born from that pain and that fight.

It seeks to expose the silent, calculated mechanisms that cults use to manipulate and isolate. But beyond that, it is the story of a mother's unrelenting pursuit of truth, justice, and the reclamation of her daughter's freedom, not just from a physical place, but from a psychological prison.

The journey has been long. The road, often lonely. But along the way, I've encountered unexpected kindness, unwavering support from strangers, and divine interventions that reminded me I was never truly alone. Each of these became a lifeline, helping me endure and believe again.

If you are reading this and fighting any battle, I want you to know: you are not alone. Let these pages be your companion, your strength, your mirror. I hope this book raises awareness, sparks vigilance, and above all, reinforces the power of love, a force more powerful than any darkness.

With all my heart,
Sanmaatrika

Acknowledgements

This book would not have been possible without the unwavering support, kindness, and strength of many beautiful souls who stood by me when the world around me seemed to fall apart.

To those divine souls who appeared like angels in the darkest chapters of my life, your help, your shelter, and your care came without expectations, and your presence reminded me that God's grace often walks the earth in human form. I may not mention your names, but your impact lives on every page of this story.

To the officers, legal aides, and silent well-wishers who extended a hand, a kind word, or simply listened without judgment, thank you for doing your part in this journey of truth.

To the hearts that whispered prayers for me, though unaware of my journey, know that your kindness found its way to me

Gratitude Beyond Words: To The Arms That Held Me:

In my darkest hours, it was God's grace that held me, and He did so through the love and strength of my family.

When the weight of my struggles became too heavy to bear, I turned to my family, the one constant I knew I could lean on. In my moments of deepest despair, their love and support became the anchor that kept me grounded.

First, my sister and brother-in-law came to Delhi. I had informed them of my daughter's departure, and they arrived within days. They stayed with me for a week, offering emotional support, advice, and compassion. When it became clear that there were no immediate actions we could take and that the journey ahead would be long, I asked them to return home. I assured them that I would manage on my own, but their presence had already strengthened my resolve.

At a time when I was once again overwhelmed by emotions and drowning in a sense of utter helplessness, my brother, living thousands of miles away in the USA, sensed the depth of my despair. Without a moment's hesitation, he put everything on hold; his work, his life, and booked the earliest possible ticket to fly to India. Within days, he was by my side. His steady presence gave me the strength I had started to lose. He accompanied me to every meeting, every court hearing, and every appointment, not just as a support but as a silent warrior walking beside me. His quiet determination, calm presence, and unwavering companionship reminded me that I was not alone. With him by my side, I found the strength to face each storm with renewed courage and hope.

My bhabhi supported his decision wholeheartedly. From the moment they heard my plight, they worked together, she coordinating logistics from afar, he offering emotional strength in person. Their partnership underscored the collective power of family.

Although my parents and sisters could not be there physically, their support was just as steadfast. My parents called daily to check that I was eating, resting, and taking care of myself. Their prayers and words of encouragement felt like a warm embrace across the miles. My sisters messaged and rang me throughout each day, sharing humor, advice, and reminders of the inner strength they knew I possessed.

Together, their collective love formed a safety net beneath me. They reminded me of who I am, a mother who would not back down, a daughter and sister who carries the strength of her family's love. Their belief in me fueled my own belief that I could overcome anything. In their support, I found the courage to face each new day, step by step, even when the road ahead seemed impossibly long.

Each of you, in your own way, became the arms that held me, the voices that encouraged me, and the light that guided me through the darkest tunnel, reminding me that even in solitude, I was never truly alone. I carry your love, care, and blessings in every step of this journey.

With heartfelt gratitude,
Sanmaatrika

CHAPTER I

A Perfect World Shattered!

A perfect world can shatter in a single moment, and in its place, only questions remain.

Laaddo (my daughter) told me about her college trip just a day before she left for the hostel and asked for ₹4,500 to cover the trip expenses. Trusting her completely, I handed over the money without hesitation. The next morning, **November 28, 2023**, she called out to me from the door as I was taking a bath.

"Maa, I'm leaving now," .

"You should've told me earlier!" I shouted from the bathroom. "I could've finished my bath after you left."

"Love you, Maa. Bye!" she said with a cheerful smile, her voice echoing in the corridor.

After about ten minutes, something unusual happened. Laaddo came back home. She had left her luggage at the corner of the main road where she'd been waiting for her college bus. She called me downstairs, and as I came down, I saw her walking towards me, her eyes heavy, emotions she rarely showed now spilling through. Before I could ask her anything, **she rushed forward and wrapped her arms around me in a tight hug**.

"Take care, Maa..." she said softly, her voice trembling slightly.

It was a heartfelt moment, but I didn't think much of it. We often shared affectionate gestures like this before parting. I smiled, told her to stay safe, and watched as she walked back towards the road. **That hug... that moment... was her way of saying goodbye to a world she once belonged to... My perfect world.**

*****

My Laaddo and I shared an unbreakable bond for as long as I can remember. To start with my story, I am a single mother, dedicated to raising my child all my life, watching her grow every day. She was not just my child but my best friend, confidant, inspiration, and the center of my world. Her radiant smile could brighten even the darkest days. Her kind and caring behavior earned her admiration from everyone who knew her.

In May 2013, I chose to walk away from my marriage and his family, embracing the strength it took to raise my child as a single mother. It was then that I resolved to take full responsibility for her and vowed to give her a better life. The road ahead wasn't easy, but the journey was worth it; a beautiful world full of meaningful challenges shared with my adorable daughter and our "unbreakable" bond.

But... was it UNBREAKABLE? Is it UNBREAKABLE?

After the separation, I worked tirelessly to establish an independent position in society. I began by taking up a private job in 2015, but it required me to stay away from my daughter and didn't pay enough to meet our needs.

My daughter had a deep understanding of our financial situation. She never demanded anything expensive, even when she truly liked something. If I ever tried to buy her something beyond our means, she would gently refuse, saying, "Maa, I don't need that. Let's not waste money on it; I'll manage without it." Her maturity and thoughtfulness left me in awe time and again, reminding me that she wasn't just my daughter, she was my greatest blessing.

Unable to bear the distance and continuous compromises, I resigned and redirected my efforts toward finding a more stable and fulfilling career. Determined to provide emotional and financial stability, I prepared for competitive exams for government jobs and eventually secured a position as a teacher at a state government residential school in 2018.

However, even in that role, the exhaustive duty hours left me feeling that I still wasn't giving my daughter the attention she deserved. With renewed determination, I set my sights on a central government teaching position that would offer a better work-life balance. After a year of relentless effort, in September 2019, I secured the role. My daughter was with me in the same school until she completed her 12th grade in 2023 and then joined college to pursue a design course. Since her college was about 30 kilometers from our home, the daily commute was exhausting, with the added pressure of college work. We mutually decided she would stay in the hostel and visit home on weekends.

Every step of this journey was fueled by my deepest desire to see my Laaddo live a joyful and fulfilling life. My dreams for her extended far beyond academic success. She truly became the kind-hearted soul I had always envisioned, someone who carried happiness within herself and shared it effortlessly. She was the kind of a daughter others only dreamed of: thoughtful, selfless, and full of life. Her handmade cards, heartfelt gifts, and spontaneous acts of love were constant reminders of her beautiful spirit. I was her protector, guide, and anchor; she was my greatest source of joy and pride.

We were a team, navigating life's ups and downs together. She would hold my hand while walking down the street, insisting my safety was more important than hers. When I struggled to lift something heavy, she would step in, lifting more than her share to ease my burden. She loved shopping for little things to brighten our home and cherished the simple moments we shared.

She was my motivation, my purpose, and my light. Everything I did was for her, and I took immense pride in the bond we shared, a bond I believed nothing could ever break.

But the perfect world we had built began to crack somewhere along the way. At first, the changes were so subtle I barely noticed. She grew quieter and more introspective, spending long hours on her phone and laptop. What worried me more was how she gradually started pulling away from family activities. The little moments we used to share: meals, movies, even weekend shopping trips, became rare. "I'm just tired," she'd say, or, "I have so much work to finish."

At first, I assumed it was just a phase: a typical teenage fascination with technology. Her conversations seemed harmless, often about spiritual practices and philosophies she had started exploring. As her mother, I trusted her judgment and believed this interest reflected her curiosity about the world beyond the material.

The shift became more apparent during visits to my hometown or family get-togethers. She often gravitated toward my cousins, who had long been involved in a so-called spiritual organization named "**Adhyatmik Ishwariya Vishwa Vidyalaya" (AIVV)**. They were my cousins, not hers, yet they had a magnetic pull on her. She would sit with them for hours, listening intently to their discussions about spirituality, enlightenment, and the supposed greater truths of life.

To me, it appeared harmless at that time. I thought, "What's wrong with learning about spirituality? Isn't that what we all strive for in some way?" How wrong I was!

My cousins, whom I believed to be well-meaning, were planting seeds of ideology strong enough to pull my daughter away from me. Their words were coated in sweet promises of peace and salvation, but underneath lay the roots of manipulation and control.

Her attachment to them deepened over time. I convinced myself it was just familial bonding. I didn't see how she was becoming emotionally dependent on their approval. In hindsight, I realize how skillfully they wove their ideas into her thoughts, subtly making her question her current life and long for something "greater." They often spoke of liberation from worldly attachments. Though I found their words idealistic and impractical, I dismissed them as harmless musings.

Her behavior at home began to change. She became more secretive, retreating to her room under the guise of studying or watching something online. I didn't question her then, trusting her implicitly. I believed our bond was unbreakable, that she would confide in me if something were truly wrong. But as I reflect on those days, I realize how much she had already begun to drift away, caught in a web of ideology slowly wrapping around her.

My cousins were not strangers to us. They had always been a part of family gatherings. But I now see how their involvement in AIVV gave them a sense of purpose they eagerly shared, especially with my daughter. They weren't content following their path alone; they sought to bring others along, believing it their "duty" to spread this so-called "truth."

What I didn't realize then was how subtly their influence was altering Laaddo's perception of the world. She began speaking of detachment, the emptiness of material pursuits, and the belief that true happiness could only be found through spiritual surrender. These were the first signs of a shift; small cracks in the life we had built together, once centered around love, trust, and mutual support.

One powerful way they isolate followers is by controlling food. They claimed the vibrations of the person cooking transfer into the food. Considering themselves spiritually pure, they avoid anything made by outsiders. My daughter never rejected the food I prepared, but strictly avoided onion and garlic. To keep her close, I adjusted my cooking for her. She always refused even a bite of food offered by neighbors or friends, not even out of courtesy.

In our culture, food is more than nourishment. It's love and care expressed through flavor and shared moments. Families bond over meals, emotions are shared in silence through warm plates, and relationships are nurtured with every bite. By instilling fear and spiritual superiority, they cut off this natural emotional connection, replacing warmth with distance and love with control.

She grew distant, though subtly, and I attributed it to her growing up and seeking space. But the space between us wasn't independence. It was a void created by invisible forces pulling her deeper into their grasp.

She was taught that this yuga, the current era, was full of suffering. Her struggles and mine were used as proof. They pointed to natural calamities as signs of the world's decay. Most dangerously, they convinced her that their so-called baba, **Virendra Dev Dixit (VDD)**, was a divine incarnation sent to guide followers from the suffering of Kalyuga to the promised Satyuga.

Despite the growing distance, she never stopped showing love in little ways. She still held my hand while sleeping, looked out for me on the road, and surprised me with thoughtful gestures. But beneath the surface, something had shifted.

I told myself that everything was fine, that this was just a phase. I had no reason to suspect otherwise. My world felt secure, our bond unshaken. I was blissfully unaware of the storm brewing, the storm that would tear my daughter away from me.

And then one day, **my perfect world shattered.**

****

CHAPTER II

When Trust Turned Blind

Not all storms come with thunder; some arrive as whispers, soft enough to be missed until everything has changed.

I remember when my Laaddo was about six years old, she once took an eraser from a friend without letting her know. I could sense it wasn't hers, but she didn't confess. Around the same time, there was a story going around town about a child who had died after being struck by lightning. That day, she asked me how that child had died. To teach her a lesson, I told her, "He had stolen an eraser from his friend, and God punished him with lightning." She was terrified by what she heard. Tears welled up in her eyes as she cried and promised to return the eraser, pleading with God not to punish her.

She was convinced that God could hear even her thoughts. It kept her innocent and truthful in childhood, but today, that same fear has taken a darker shape. She's scared even to question or doubt the ideology she's following. She wasn't lost; she's trapped, held captive by the same fear of divine punishment, blindly following what she believes is God's will.

It started with her growing fascination with spiritual ideas. As a young child, she had always been curious about life and the universe, asking questions that often left me speechless.

"What happens after we die, Maa?",

"Where do people go?",

"Do they come back?" she would ask, her wide, innocent eyes searching for answers.

At the time, I brushed off her questions with simple reassurances or vague explanations, assuming that her curiosity would fade as she grew older. But it didn't fade. As a teenager, her questions became more frequent and profound. She wanted to know about the soul, karma, and the purpose of life. I now regret not engaging with her on these topics more deeply. I didn't see what I see so clearly now. Those unanswered questions became a fertile ground for others to step in and provide their own interpretations, persuasive answers that would eventually lead her away from me.

Her increased time spent on her phone and laptop was another red flag I missed. She seemed to be engrossed in something, always watching videos, reading, or chatting online. When I'd ask her what she was doing, she'd respond casually, *"Just watching something, Maa. Don't worry."* Her tone was so light, her expression so normal, that I didn't press further. I trusted her completely, never imagining that she could be exposed to harmful influences right within the safety of our home.

My cousins, who had long been followers of AIVV, spoke with such conviction about their practices, their guru, and their beliefs that I found it hard to challenge them. I didn't think much of their influence at first. To me, they were family, and family was supposed to look out for each other.

During those visits to my hometown, my daughter would spend hours with them, listening intently to their discussions. They spoke about liberation from material attachments, the promise of eternal happiness, and the importance of surrendering oneself to a higher purpose. Their words were laced with authority, and they carried an air of certainty that seemed to captivate her.

At home, she started echoing their teachings, often questioning the purpose of worldly attachments and routines. One day, she asked me with a newfound intensity:

"Maa, why do people say we should follow spirituality only after retirement?"

"What if we die suddenly before retirement?"

"When will we get connected to God if we're occupied with worldly responsibilities until our last breath?"

It wasn't the kind of query she would have asked before. I tried to explain with the patience and love of a mother.

"Laaddo, God has sent us to this earth with duties assigned for every stage of life. Fulfilling those duties is a part of being grateful to Him. Just as parents want their children to focus on studies while at school, it doesn't mean they forget their parents. However, during school hours, their focus needs to remain on their lessons. In the same way, we can stay connected to God while fulfilling our worldly responsibilities."

But I could sense that my words didn't resonate with her. Her mind was already being conditioned by the teachings of my cousins and AIVV, their messages far stronger and more persistent than mine. My explanations seemed to pale in comparison to the relentless influence they were exerting over her, and I couldn't help but feel an ache of helplessness as I watched her drift further away.

Her dedication to dressing neatly and maintaining a polished appearance not only reflected her disciplined nature and attention to detail but also showcased her vibrant spirit and enthusiastic approach to life.

Her teachers often appreciated her for her diligence and commitment, qualities that set her apart. But the influence of my cousins and AIVV began to overshadow these traits. They instilled in her the belief that traditional school and college education was merely *"Dogly"* education, trivial and meaningless in comparison to their so-called *"Godly"* teachings.

Gradually, their manipulation took hold, convincing her that the pursuit of academic knowledge was futile. As a result, she abandoned her college education midway through her first-semester exams, walking away from a path she had worked so hard to build, only to immerse herself entirely in their ideology.

She was curious, and curiosity was healthy, wasn't it? I saw no harm in her spending time with them. If anything, I thought it was better than her wasting time on meaningless pursuits.

My cousins encouraged her to read their baba's teachings, attend online sessions, and participate in discussions. They praised her for her interest, telling her she was wise beyond her age and destined for a higher purpose, "a chosen one".

She became increasingly withdrawn, spending less time with me and more time alone. Our conversations, once filled with laughter and shared dreams, grew shorter and more strained. When I tried to engage her, she seemed distracted, her mind elsewhere. The warmth in her eyes and the spark that used to light up her face were gone, replaced by a guarded, distant expression.

Our conversations became infrequent and indifferent. I was desperate; she had grown cold.

I once told her, *"I miss the daughter you used to be. Even though you're right here beside me, it feels like I've lost you."*

And in her detached tone came a reply that pierced deeper than silence:

"I regret being so good before; that's why you're irritating me now and expecting me to stay the same."

Her response left me shattered. Her words cut through me like a dagger, leaving me stunned and heartbroken. It wasn't just what she said but the conviction in her voice that made me realize how deeply she had changed. The daughter I knew, the one who was my pillar of strength, seemed like a distant memory.

Even when she was right there beside me, I couldn't shake the feeling of being alone. The place that once radiated the warmth of our love now felt cold and distant. But despite the emptiness that lingered, I found solace in knowing she was safe, right in front of me. There was a strange comfort in that, even if it didn't seem like enough. I told myself it was just a phase, a momentary lull. I believed with every ounce of my being that there would be more chances, more moments, to rekindle the spark and breathe life back into what we once shared. I held on to that certainty, trusting that the bond we built was stronger than the distance.

As the days passed, the distance between us seemed to grow quietly but steadily. I began to notice the subtle shifts; how she spent increasing hours on her phone, the constant glow of the screen silently replacing our conversations.

Even late into the night, she would remain glued to her laptop, always busy, always immersed in her work. Often, exhaustion would silently overtake her, and she would fall asleep without even realizing it. The laptop would still be on, casting a faint glow on her tired face.

Sometimes, I'd wake up in the middle of the night and find her lying on the mat, shivering without a bedsheet, no pillow under her head, completely unaware of her own discomfort. Quietly, I would place a pillow beneath her and gently cover her with a bedsheet, tucking her in with a silent prayer for her well-being.

I would ask her gently, but she began to see my concern as nagging. Her growing secrecy began to frighten me. Those were the moments when worry stopped being a passing thought and began to settle in my heart as something heavier, something painfully real.

Was this just a phase?

Or had she unwittingly trapped herself in something far bigger than I could understand, something I couldn't pull her out of?

****

CHAPTER III

When Love Meets Deception

*The worst thing about betrayal is that it never comes from
your enemies.*

What made things worse was the arrival of **Amol**, the lawyer of **AIVV**, into their circle in 2022. My cousins might not have been so harmful had he not entered their lives and manipulated both them and my daughter. **I had no idea that Laaddo was in regular touch with Amol until after she left home.** Even my cousins encouraged her to stay connected with him, further strengthening his influence over her.

She had been made to lock all her WhatsApp conversations with the people involved in this ideology, and even renamed their contacts using the names of her school or college friends and faculty members. The seeds of change were being sown back then—seeds that would eventually grow into a divide so deep, I could never have imagined it. What I had assumed were innocent chats and harmless curiosity were, in fact, the beginnings of a manipulation that would one day take my Laaddo away from me.

***

The day Laaddo left home is etched in my memory like a wound that refuses to heal. It was the culmination of weeks of subtle changes, covert plans, and manipulation so strong that even her love for me couldn't withstand it.

On **November 28, 2023**, I didn't sense the storm brewing. I was still blind to the gravity of the situation, trusting her completely as I always had.

Before leaving for college, she returned home from the main road where she had left her luggage, hugged me, and said goodbye — showing her love and internal conflict.

That hug lingered in my heart long after she let go. For a few seconds, time stood still, as if the universe wanted me to hold on to her a little longer. She didn't say much. Her voice was soft, almost trembling, when she said, "Maa, I just felt like coming back to hug you once more." Then, with a brave smile that masked her inner turmoil, she turned away and walked back toward the main road.

I stood there at the gate, watching her small frame grow distant. Something in her steps felt unusually heavy that day. It was as if she was carrying a burden far beyond her years. I didn't know then that this simple goodbye hid behind it a web of lies, conditioning, and manipulation she herself hadn't fully understood.

She had already decided to leave and to never return. But something in her heart, something pure and untouched, had brought her back for that one final hug; a silent cry from the daughter I once knew.

And I? I had no idea that moment was the last trace of her, the girl I had raised, before the cult swallowed her entirely.

Two days later, on **December 1**, instead of her college trip, she left for Delhi. She rang me casually that morning, gently reminding me again about the trip. There was a quiet calm in the way she packed her bags-as if everything was just as it should be. Around 8:45 a.m., she left her hostel by booking a cab and headed straight to the railway station, where one of Amol's followers was already waiting to accompany her to Delhi. Their train was scheduled for 9:00 p.m.

During the day, they visited a nearby post office and posted several pre-drafted letters to nearby police stations. These letters falsely claimed that she was leaving home of her own free will and sought protection from me. This was all part of a meticulously planned strategy by the cult leader, Amol, to permanently sever her ties with me.

The next few days that followed were a whirlwind of confusion and heartbreak. Her communication during her journey had been sparse, with excuses of low battery or being too busy to talk. On **December 3**, I called her, hoping to confirm that she had returned from the trip. When a woman answered through her phone and addressed me as *"Mataji,"* a term I instantly recognized from my cousins' spiritual jargon, my heart froze. The call was abruptly cut off when the woman realized her mistake. Desperately, I redialed 10-15 times, unable to contain my panic. Finally, I received a text message from my daughter, saying she had just reached her hostel and was holding her luggage, so she couldn't talk immediately. She assured me she would call back in 30 minutes.

As promised, she called me after half an hour and spoke as if nothing unusual had happened. Her voice was warm and cheerful, and she even described how much she had enjoyed the trip. Her calm demeanour and seemingly normal tone made me question my instincts, but deep inside, something still felt terribly wrong.

That evening, around 9:30 PM, I called her again. She answered, speaking normally, but when I switched to a video call, she hesitated.

"My roommates are tired, Maa. They're sleeping, and the lights are off," she said. I insisted she step outside, and then reluctantly, she accepted the video call.

The moment I saw her, I understood something was off. The background wasn't her hostel room. There was a curtain behind her, something her hostel didn't have. My heart raced. *"Where are you?"* I demanded. She continued to talk as if everything was normal, but her body language betrayed her. After ending the call, I messaged her to share her location. Panicked, she tried to stall, even calling a friend to retrieve her hostel's location. When she finally sent a location from Google Maps, I knew it was fake. She wasn't at her hostel.

When I confronted her, she admitted the truth: she was in Delhi. My world shattered. I yelled, *"How could you lie to me?"* Her voice trembled, but her resolve was firm.

Even then, I thought she might have gone to attend any of their spiritual programs and would return in a day or two. I planned to talk to her when she came back, unaware that **she had left me, never intending to return.**

The following morning, **December 4**, I received an email with the subject line, ***"Meri baat suno, Maa."*** It was from my daughter. My hands trembled as I clicked it open. The email was a heartbreaking mix of scripted assurances and emotional appeals.

"Maa mujhe spirituality me interest hai... Mai isiko follow karna chaahti hun.... Agar mein bolke Delhi aati to mujhe pakka pata tha ki aap aane nahi dete...Mujhe jaisa environment chaahiye waise wahan nahi mil raha hai... Isiliye bahut soch samajh kar maine ye decision liya hai... Mai itni to samjhdaar hun ki apna decision khud le sakun... Aapke liye to mai hamesha bachchi hi hun... par mere beliefs aur aapke beliefs alag hai.... aap please meri baat ko samjhiye... Mai bilkul sahi raste par jaa rahi hun... ye rasta mere liye bilkul theek hai...

I'm happy.
I've found my
spiritual path.

Mai apni marzi se hi yahan Delhi aai hu... Mujhe yahan accha lagta hai... Main adhyatmikta me hi sewa karna chaahti hun...

Mera timetable set hoga... khana sahi se khaungi... Bahut kuch sikhne milega... bahut safe aur achchi jagah par hun... Darne ki koi baat hi nahi hai... Apna dhyan rakhna... Jyada time nahi hai... jaldi milenge... Hostel me bas thoda sa saman hai aur matress hai... aaram se le aana.... Aap bhi meri khushi hi chahte ho na... Apko pata hi tha mujhe yahan kab se aana tha... Mai yahan pe bahut khush hun... Aap bhi khush rehna... Apna dhyan rakhna... Sorry maa abhi aapko bura lagega lekin baad me aap khud bologe ki sahi kaam ki hun. Dekhna ek din aap yahan khud aaoge... Aapko pakka vishwas hoga...dekhna aap..

Maa aap mujhse pyar karte ho to please mujhe jo pasand hai vo karne do.... Mujhe college ki life pasand nahi hai aur naa hi mai shaadi karna chaahti hun... Aap tension mat lo mai yahan bahut khush hun... Apna dhyan rakhna...

Om Shanti.
Aapki beti"

English Translation:

"Maa... I'm interested in spirituality, and I want to follow this path. If I had told you and come to Delhi, I knew for sure that you wouldn't have allowed it. I wasn't getting the kind of environment I needed back there. That's why, after giving it a lot of thought, I made this decision. I'm mature enough now to make my own decisions. I know that to you, I'll always be your little girl, but my beliefs are different from yours. Please try to understand me. I'm walking along the right path, and this path feels right for me. I've come to Delhi entirely by my own choice, and I feel happy here. I want to dedicate myself to serving through spirituality.

I'll have a proper routine, eat well, and learn so many things. I'm in a safe and good place; there's absolutely nothing to worry about. Please take care of yourself. We'll meet soon; it won't be long. There's just a little stuff and a mattress left at the hostel. You can bring it easily. You too want my happiness, don't you? You already knew I'd been wanting to come here for a long time. I'm truly happy here. You also be happy and take care of yourself."

"I'm sorry, Maa. I know this hurts you now, but one day you'll say that I made the right choice. You'll see, one day, you'll come here yourself, and you'll also believe in this, I'm sure of it. Maa, if you really love me, then please let me do what brings me joy. I don't like college life, and I don't want to get married. Please don't worry, I'm very happy here. Take care of yourself.

Om Shanti.
Your Daughter "

I read her words over and over, trying to make sense of them. One line stood out like a cruel joke: **Hostel mei bas thoda sa saman hai aur mattress hai... Aram se le aana.** My heart sank as I realized what she meant. She wasn't planning to return home.

I called her immediately, begging her to come back, but her tone was resolute. *"I won't come back, Maa,"* she said. *"This is my path now."* I broke down, shouting that I would bring her back no matter what.

Later that day, a registered letter arrived at my address. It was addressed to the police but was mistakenly sent to my home. In it, my daughter declared that she had left of her own free will and requested police protection from me, accusing me of trying to force her back. I felt a wave of disbelief and despair. My daughter had never posted a letter in her life and didn't even know how to format one. Someone guided her.

On **December 4**, during one of my desperate attempts to gather support, I contacted my cousin, the same person who had introduced my daughter to the cult. That was when I learned something that shook me to my core: her own daughter, Nisha, a 35-year-old IT professional, had also willingly joined the same cult just months earlier. The very people I had once trusted had not only misled my daughter but had allowed their own family to be drawn into the same trap.

I begged my cousin for help, hoping she'd persuade her daughter to intervene. But my pleas were met with indifference. *"Your daughter's decision was her own,"* she said coldly. Her refusal to acknowledge her role in this nightmare felt like another betrayal.

Late at night, desperate for answers, I turned to her old laptop. Searching through her email sent folder, I found the same mail she had sent to multiple police stations, including one to the DCP of South-West Delhi, which was just a 3hours after I spoke with her. Her email accused me of threatening her and pleaded for police protection. It was clear these words weren't hers but those of Amol, the cult leader and lawyer guiding her every move.

A silent scream echoed inside me. The pain of seeing those emails was overwhelming. My daughter, my honest, loving child, who once couldn't bear to see me upset, had been manipulated into turning against me. But it was the realization that she had been coached and instructed to fabricate lies against me that broke me entirely. But even in the face of this betrayal, I couldn't bring myself to blame her. She was a victim as much as I was; just a pawn in a game orchestrated by people who preyed on innocence and trust.

On **5th December**, I boarded an evening flight to Delhi. Late that night, I landed at the airport, my heart heavy with a mix of fear and determination. Immediately upon arrival, the lady in charge and her husband received me, smiling, polite, doing their best to appear welcoming, and escorted me to their residence. At 2 AM, once we reached their home, I asked to see Laaddo. She told me, firmly, that I couldn't meet her until morning because of their "rules." Exhausted and broken, I waited through the night, clinging to the hope that with the dawn, I could finally bring my daughter back.

What followed was the most emotionally harrowing experience of my life.

****

CHAPTER IV

A Stranger in My Daughter's Skin

It is easier to fool people than to convince them that they have been fooled.

The realization that my daughter was involved in a cult struck me like a bolt of lightning. It felt as though the world I had carefully built around us was crumbling, brick by brick. There had been signs: small, almost imperceptible changes in her behavior, but I had dismissed them, attributing them to teenage rebellion or a passing phase. Little did I know, the reality was far more sinister.

On **December 6, 2023**, after a sleepless night, I was desperate to see her and understand what was happening. That morning, I entered the so-called *ashram's* second floor where she was staying. It didn't feel like a spiritual place; it felt more like a prison. Curtains covered every entrance, iron grills on all sides, and locks on every floor. After reaching there, I wasn't taken to her directly. I had to wait and pass through four locked doors, one after another, before I could see my Laaddo.

She finally entered the stark, bare room, and for a moment, I forgot how to breathe. The girl who stood before me looked like my Laaddo, but everything else felt wrong. Her body was stiff, her movements mechanical. The sparkle in her eyes, once so full of laughter and curiosity, had vanished, replaced by an eerie emptiness. Her face, once so expressive, was now unreadable, frozen in a mask of detachment. She spoke, but her voice was flat, as if echoing someone else's script. The warmth, the softness, the soul I had known so intimately... it was as if it had all been erased. She was here, yet so far away. Like a stranger wearing my child's skin.

"Our karmic account as mother and daughter is cleared," she said flatly. *"I am free to choose my path now."*

All my words hit an impenetrable wall. *"Laaddo, I'm here for you,"* I said, trying to reach her. *"Let's go home and talk this through. Whatever is troubling you, we can solve it together."*

She shook her head slowly. *"Maa, you don't understand. This is my life now. I've chosen this path."* It was rehearsed.

Tears brimmed in my eyes, unspoken pain rising to the surface as I reached for her hand, but she recoiled. *"Don't, Maa,"* she whispered. *"Touching me disturbs my vibrations."*

Her words stung more than any physical blow ever could. The daughter who once clung to me while we walked together, who would hug me tightly before falling asleep, now flinched at my touch.

Each word pierced my heart like a dagger. These were not her words; they were implanted by someone else, designed to sever the bond we shared. I tried to reason with her, to remind her of our love, our memories, and our dreams. But she remained unmoved, her responses calculated and devoid of warmth. The cult had succeeded in creating a barrier between us, and for the first time, I felt completely helpless.

During our conversation, I mentioned a cherished memory from her childhood, a handmade birthday card she had lovingly created for me. For a split second, her eyes softened, and I saw a glimmer of the girl I knew. But the moment passed as quickly as it had appeared. She straightened her back, shook her head slightly, and said, *"Maa, you must understand that I'm on a different path now."*

Her face remained stoic, but I noticed her hands trembling slightly. She quickly folded them in her lap, as if to regain control. The brief flicker of emotion gave me a shred of hope, but it also underscored the depth of her conditioning.

As she stood to leave, I instinctively reached out, unable to hold back.

"Laaddo, please... just think about everything once more. Come back home," I whispered, my voice trembling with hope and desperation.

She paused just for a heartbeat and looked at me.

"I'm happy here. You should be, too," she said, her tone eerily calm.

There was no warmth in her words, no trace of conflict in her expression, just an unsettling stillness. And then she turned away, slipping back into that haunting silence, leaving me in the suffocating depth of that silence.

The weight of that encounter bore down on me as I left the place. My daughter was physically present, but emotionally, she felt unreachable. I replayed every word, every expression, searching for clues, for hope, for anything that could tell me she was still my daughter underneath it all.

*****

My second visit to those premises was accompanied by the police, a step I had to take. It took me three days of persistent visits to the police station, spending mornings to evenings explaining my plight and pleading for help. Only then did the officers accompany me to the ashram. Each day of waiting and explaining felt endless, but I knew I couldn't give up. My daughter's safety and freedom depended on my persistence. I had hoped that the presence of law enforcement would cut through the barriers that the cult had erected, but even this visit was fraught with resistance and manipulation.

As we approached the place, the atmosphere was thick with tension. The police officers, led by a female Sub-Inspector (SI), requested entry, but the AIVV members were relentless in their obstruction. They claimed that my daughter was there of her own free will and insisted that no intervention was necessary. Their arguments were laced with confidence that seemed rehearsed, as though they had faced similar situations before and knew how to deflect them.

It took several attempts and persistent negotiation from the SI before they finally allowed us inside. However, their compliance was far from genuine. Once inside, my daughter was brought out, but she wasn't alone. A group of cult followers surrounded her, acting as an impenetrable wall of influence and control. Their presence was intimidating, and their eyes never left her, as though silently warning her against saying anything they hadn't approved.

The SI attempted to speak with her, but she wasn't permitted to talk freely. Every question was met with guarded responses, her words carefully measured. She appeared more like a puppet than the strong-willed girl I had raised. The followers hovered around her, cutting off any chance of a private conversation.

Finally, they coerced her into writing a statement declaring that she was an adult now and had come to this so-called ashram of her own volition. Watching her write those words, surrounded by the very people who had manipulated her, was one of the most helpless moments of my life. The police, bound by procedure, had no choice but to accept her written statement.

As we left the premises that day, my heart felt heavier than ever. The sight of my daughter, so visibly controlled and unable to express her true feelings, haunted me. That visit made it painfully clear how deeply she was entangled in their web and how determined they were to keep her under their control.

*****

My third and fourth visits to this place remain etched in my memory as some of the most heart-wrenching experiences of this journey. Each visit felt like stepping into a battlefield, armed only with hope and a mother's unwavering love, but I was met with cruelty, manipulation, and relentless obstruction.On my third visit, I arrived determined to see my daughter and ensure her safety. As I approached the so-called ashram, I found the gates locked, presenting an eerie, unwelcoming silence. It was as if the entire building had been abandoned. The biting cold cut through me like a blade, chilling me to the bone and making it hard to stand still.

Despite the freezing wind numbing my fingers and face, I stood outside for hours, calling out Laaddo, hoping for any sign of her. I knocked on the gates repeatedly, my hands, my fingers shook, numbed by the chill of the metal, but there was no response.

After an endless wait, a girl peered out from the door behind the locked grills and curtains and said, *"One minute,"* before disappearing. I waited anxiously, my heart pounding with a mix of desperation and hope. But minutes turned into hours, and no one came back. The cold was unbearable, seeping into every part of my body, making even breathing feel painful. With each passing moment, my fears deepened. I screamed her name, pleading for her to come out, to let me know she was safe. My cries echoed in the frigid air, unanswered.

For over three hours, I stood there, shivering uncontrollably, my voice hoarse, tears freezing on my cheeks. The relentless cold was unforgiving, sapping my strength, yet I couldn't leave. I felt invisible, as though my anguish didn't matter. The silence from the other side of the gates was deafening, a cruel reminder of the barriers this cult had placed between me and my daughter.

Eventually, with a heavy heart and no response, I left the place in deep disappointment.

Meanwhile, on the other side, Laaddo was being made to send an email to her college, requesting her original documents that had been submitted at the time of admission. When the college authorities called me to confirm why such a request had been made, I told them not to respond, explaining that there was a miscommunication between us. Thankfully, they followed my advice and did not act on her request. But when she didn't receive a response, she was again prompted by the cult to escalate matters. This time, she sent an email to the UGC, accusing the college of withholding her documents and refusing to return them.

*****

The next morning, when I returned for my next visit, I decided to make another attempt, hoping to catch them off guard. The followers met me with cold indifference, claiming that my daughter wasn't there. *"She has gone to Himachal Pradesh for sewa,"* they said from inside the main gate, their words laced with a casualness.

I refused to leave. My instincts told me they were lying, that my daughter was somewhere inside those walls. I pleaded, argued, and when nothing worked, I threatened to involve the local community and expose their deceit. Only then did they grudgingly allow me inside the gate.

As I stepped through the gate, they repeated their lies with a detached calm, insisting that I should be happy for her. *"You should sacrifice for her happiness,"* one follower said in a patronizing tone, as if the deep bond I share with my daughter could be so easily dismissed.

How could they ask me to celebrate the very thing that was tearing my heart apart? How could they expect me to accept their lies as truth, to abandon my Laaddo to their control?

Every interaction was a calculated attempt to manipulate me, to make me doubt myself and the unbreakable bond I share with my Laaddo. Yet their tactics only fueled my determination. I wasn't there to appease them or to accept their false narrative. I was there for my daughter, and no number of locked gates, lies, or cold indifference could shake me to bring her back.

In the days that followed, the full weight of what had happened began to sink in. My Laaddo, my only child, had been manipulated into believing that she needed to distance herself from me to achieve spiritual enlightenment. The thought of her being under the influence of people who cared nothing for her well-being haunted me day and night.

The helplessness was overwhelming. I had always been her protector, her guide, her anchor. Now, I felt powerless against the forces that had taken her from me. I cried myself to sleep every night, praying for strength, clarity, and a way to bring her back.

But that first meeting was a turning point for me. It awakened a fierce determination to fight for my daughter, no matter the odds. I knew that the road ahead would be fraught with challenges, but I was ready to face them all. My love for her was my guiding light, and I clung to the hope that **she would one day return to me**, free from the grip of the cult.

Although the image of her lifeless expression stayed with me, my instincts as a mother echoed that she needed me most, even if she couldn't see it. I stayed in Delhi for around six months, putting my life on hold. Those months were filled with relentless efforts to gather evidence, piece together her story, and find a way to bring her back. It was a period of anguish and determination, a battle for her freedom, her happiness, and her soul.

The fleeting moments of emotion I had seen in her eyes reminded me that my daughter was still there, beneath the layers of conditioning. I vowed to fight for her with every ounce of strength I had left. I knew the journey ahead would be long and arduous, but my love for her would never waver.

While I was feeling helpless and lost, there were moments in my journey that I can only describe as miraculous. One evening, I was wandering into the area where my daughter was residing to inquire about a vacant house for rent. The landlady, a kind-hearted woman, who heard about my situation from her neighbor, asked me if I had eaten that day. I didn't. Such was the weight of my pain that I had completely forgotten about my hunger. Her concern melted through my despair, and she insisted that I have a meal. She served me warm, delicious food and treated me like family, her kindness wrapping around me like a comforting embrace. Her generosity wasn't just about the food; it reminded me that even in the darkest times, there are people who care deeply for others, even strangers.

With renewed energy, I continued the path of a grueling battle, one that would test the limits of my courage and resilience. But for my daughter, I was ready to face anything. She was my life, my purpose, and my greatest love. ***No force on earth could stop me from bringing her back home.***

****

CHAPTER V

Delhi Diaries: From Darkness to Determination

Courage is not the absence of fear, but rather the judgment that something else is more important than fear.

Every step in Delhi felt like wading through quicksand. As I tried to understand the forces at work, I uncovered pieces of the puzzle that made my stomach churn. The registered letters, the emails, the scripted conversations, they were all part of a sinister plan orchestrated by Amol and his cult, AIVV.

Staying in Delhi wasn't a choice; it was a necessity. For around six months, I remained in the city, leaving my own path in the hope of guiding hers back. A friend's brother, a beacon of humanity during my darkest hours, graciously offered me shelter.

Their family was already navigating their own set of challenges, yet they welcomed me without hesitation. They didn't just provide me with a place to stay; they offered me a sense of belonging in a city where I felt like a stranger. It was in their home, surrounded by kindness and support, that I found the strength to keep going.

One day, I found myself walking late at night through a desolate street on the way to the place where I was residing. The cold was biting, and nearby houses were firmly shut. There was no one ahead of me or behind me. Only my shadow kept me company, along with the sound of my own footsteps echoing in my ears, a haunting rhythm in the silence of the night. I desperately hoped to find someone to walk with, someone who might make me feel less alone. But even then, a quiet fear lingered: would such company be safe?

My fear grew as I approached a group of 10–12 barking dogs blocking the way ahead. They were about 50 meters away, and as I reached within 10 meters of them, I froze, unsure of how to proceed.

Suddenly, as if out of nowhere, a man appeared. Without a word, he drew the dogs' attention, attracting them toward him and clearing the path for me. He carried food for the dogs, which they eagerly followed, creating a safe passage for me to reach home. This wasn't an ordinary encounter; I am convinced he was an angel sent by God to protect me in that moment of vulnerability.

I stayed at my friend's brother's house for almost a month. Their kindness remained a beacon of hope during my darkest days. However, as time passed, I began to feel like an unintentional burden. Despite their unwavering hospitality, I couldn't shake the feeling that my presence might be adding to their struggles. It was then that I decided to look for another place to stay, a daunting task in a vast, unfamiliar city like Delhi.

While I was struggling to find a place to stay, a professional acquaintance unexpectedly came forward. He offered me his vacant flat without expecting anything in return. The gesture felt like another divine intervention; a reassurance that I wasn't alone in my fight. When I expressed my desire to pay for the accommodation, he firmly refused.

"This is not about money," he said. *"This is about helping someone in need."*

His words touched my heart deeply. The flat, though modest and unoccupied for a while, gave me a sense of security and stability that I desperately needed at that time.

After finding shelter, my heart told me not to waste a single moment. I ran from place to place with trembling hope, looking for someone, anyone, who could help me bring my daughter back.

The first door I knocked on was that of the Delhi Commission for Women (DCW). A kind woman who was assigned to me by DCW listened with empathy. She wanted to help. But her hands were tied; my daughter had turned 18 just 15 days ago. That one number... that one line on paper... stood between a mother's cry for help and the system's refusal to act.

I was told again and again, *"She's an adult now."*

But those who told me this didn't see the girl behind the number. A girl who had barely stepped into the world. A girl who had never been taught to doubt the voices that dressed themselves in spiritual language.

I kept moving, from one police station to another, gathering my strength, repeating my plea. And each time, I was met with the same shrug of helplessness.

"She's 18. We can't do anything."

But what the law couldn't see, a criminal did. He watched the calendar, not to protect her rights, but to plan his move. He knew exactly when her birthday was. He didn't wait because she was mature; he waited because the law would stop protecting her as a child.

And so, he timed it perfectly; not out of respect for the law, but to dance around it.

He didn't succeed because he was wise; he succeeded because the system failed; it failed to protect the most vulnerable part of our society: our trusting children, our daughters standing at the delicate threshold between childhood and adulthood. What pride is there in that? He didn't guide her into the light. He stole her away under the shadow of a loophole. He didn't give her strength. He fed her a carefully crafted story while methodically isolating her from the truth. He didn't win by right or by reason; he exploited a legal transition to commit a moral wrong. And that will never be remembered as a victory. It will be known for what it truly was: abuse, disguised as wisdom. Cowardice, masked by control.

The law may have remained silent, but this book will not. It will tell the truth that the law could not. It will expose Amol for who he truly is behind the mask of spirituality.

I took a brief pause, just long enough to breathe and collect myself. And then, I turned to the one thing that could never lie: **Technology**.

In the silence that followed her sudden disappearance, I found myself alone with my pain, but also with a quiet determination to uncover the truth. In that stillness, I turned to the digital fragments Laaddo had unknowingly left behind. Slowly, painfully, I began piecing together the puzzle from her Google account activity, WhatsApp backups, and scattered files. It felt like putting together a broken mirror; every shard reflected a fragment of the truth, and every one of them cut deep.

What I uncovered was nothing short of shock.

- **Pre-drafted letters:** She had been made to write carefully worded letters to police stations, hostel authorities, and other institutions, each letter a step toward severing herself from my care, and each crafted to portray her actions as voluntary and independent.
- **WhatsApp chats:** These revealed that she was being guided at every step by cult followers, instructed on what to say, how to behave, and how to conceal the truth from me and the outside world.
- **Fabricated email IDs:** Multiple email accounts were created in her name, used to communicate false narratives and gain approvals from her college under false pretenses.
- **Audio recordings:** I found chilling voice recordings in which she was either being coached or coerced, conversations that clearly showed how she was being mentally manipulated.
- **Video footage:** These included Amol singing Bollywood songs to lure girls, making false spiritual claims, and appearing inappropriately dressed in boxers while sitting with one of the girls, exposing his manipulative tactics and lack of genuine devotion.

And among the most painful revelations was the discovery that on **14**[th] **November 2023**, just three days before her **18**[th] birthday, she had been secretly provided with a new SIM card by one of my cousins, without my knowledge. That contact number, I later found out, belonged to one of Amol's followers and was used to maintain a secure and untraceable line of communication with the cult. Through this number, they coordinated her departure, insulated from any oversight or interference from my side. From that point forward, all her sensitive communications happened through this new number, a digital lifeline to the cult, and a dead end for a mother desperately trying to reach her child.

But the evidence I needed was there; undeniable proof that she had been manipulated, coached, and pushed into walking away from her family. Armed with evidence, truth, and the strength of a mother's heart, I finally filed a writ petition in the Delhi High Court, seeking justice and the safe return of my daughter.

It marked the beginning of my legal battle, my official fight in court. But even then, things didn't move as I expected. The court process was slow, with dates getting pushed, delays piling up, and my daughter sinking deeper into the cult's grip.

As the legal process crawled forward, I couldn't just wait. So, I began reaching out to every commission and portal that could possibly listen:

- NCPCR (National Commission for Protection of Child Rights)
- NHRC (National Human Rights Commission)
- National Commission for Women (NCW)
- Prime Minister's Grievance Portal

But one after another, I received the same disheartening reply:

""Your case is sub judice. We cannot interfere.""

Their words felt like a wall closing in on me. I had turned to those commissions not just as offices, but as beacons of hope, places where I believed a mother's voice would still be heard. But it seemed justice had rules, and none of them were written for someone like me. Yet I still held on. I had no political reach, no big name, no crowd behind me, but I had truth, a mother's love, and unshakable faith.

One late night, after a long, disheartening day filled with rejections and unanswered questions, I stepped out of the metro station, physically and emotionally drained. My mind was spinning, my feet numb, and my heart heavy, too burdened even for tears. I flagged down an auto rickshaw and gave the driver my address. Without a word, he began driving. I noticed another passenger was already seated inside, but I was too exhausted to acknowledge him. I leaned back, closed my eyes, and let the silence of the night wrap around me.

Midway through the ride, I suddenly realized I didn't have enough change to pay the fare. A wave of panic rose in my chest as I fumbled through my bag, hoping to find a few hidden coins. Just then, the man sitting opposite me, the quiet fellow passenger, calmly extended his hand toward me. In it were the exact coins I needed, already resting in his open palm, as if he had known all along that I would need them. I tried to refuse, embarrassed and overwhelmed, but he simply smiled and folded his hands in a humble gesture of goodwill.

His presence was calm, almost luminous, and his gesture felt like a balm to my anxious heart.

When we finally reached my stop, I stepped down and turned back to thank him. He remained seated, hands still folded, his gentle smile glowing softly in the dim rickshaw light as it rolled away into the night.

His simple act of kindness became a blazing reminder that even in my loneliest moments, I am never truly alone. Unseen forces, sent by a higher grace, walk beside me, guiding, comforting, and lighting the way forward with gentle compassion. In that moment, I knew he wasn't just a fellow traveler; he was a divine messenger, sent to remind me of God's presence in the most unexpected places.

These incidents were not mere coincidences. Their kindness and support gave me the strength to continue my fight. They were profound reminders that God's angels were walking alongside me, guiding me through the darkness.

****

CHAPTER VI

The Gentle Snare

It rarely begins with chains; just words soft enough to seem harmless, and firm enough to rewrite a mind.

After analyzing all the pieces of evidence, I came to understand how it all began. But reaching that clarity wasn't simple. After my daughter left home, I clung to every thread that might lead me back to her. I began going through her social media activity, saved call records, emails, and WhatsApp chat backups, anything I could access. With God's help and support from a few silent angels who crossed my path just when I needed them, I began to gather undeniable proof. Slowly, evidence surfaced: chats, voice notes, altered documents, and witness accounts. These weren't just digital files to me; they were my lifelines, which revealed the extent of brainwashing my daughter had undergone and the tactics used to sever her from me.

*****

Amol's first conversation with my daughter occurred on **September 11, 2022**, and was carefully constructed, a subtle yet deliberate attempt to draw her into his influence. He began with casual small talk, inquiring about her studies, school schedule, and language proficiency. The conversation appeared harmless, but beneath the surface, he was gathering information, mapping out her academic background, family environment, and personal interests, all while building a rapport that would make her comfortable opening up to him.

He validated her achievements by expressing admiration for her academic performance, telling her how impressive it was that she scored 94% in her 10th-grade exams. At the same time, he subtly positioned himself as an accomplished figure, mentioning his National Merit Scholarship, ensuring that she viewed him as someone knowledgeable and successful. By doing this, he established an authoritative role in her life, someone she could admire and trust.

The conversation soon took a more profound turn as he began probing into her relationship with her mother.

Amol: *Mummy kya... daant-ti rehti hai apko?*
(Does your mother scold you a lot?)

Laaddo: *Nahi... Jab matlab padhai nahi karti hun... Din bhar mai kabhi isi me lagi rehti hun to daant-ti hai...*
(No... Only when I don't study... If I spend the whole day on this(the work assigned by Amol), then she scolds me.)

Amol: *Mummy ko gyaan achcha nahi lagta hai?*
(Does your mother not like this spiritual knowledge?)

Laaddo: *Nahi... matlab... achcha lagta hai... lekin utna nishchay nahi hai*

Mummy ko abhi poora...
(No... I mean... she likes it, but she isn't completely committed yet.)

Amol: *Apko ho gaya nishchay?*
(Are you determined?)

Laaddo: *Kabhi kabhi aise... Abhi... Achcha to lagta hai... achche se karti to hun, lekinnn... Haan.... Ho gaya hai...*
(Sometimes... Right now... I like it... I follow it properly, but... yes, I'm determined now.)

In this brief exchange, he successfully planted the idea that my uncertainty was a shortcoming, subtly encouraging her to see herself as more devoted. By questioning her faith, he pushed her to prove her commitment, making her feel like she needed to be firmer in her belief than her mother.

Amol:*Abhi padhai to sabhi padh rahe hai na.. wo saare engineering... engineers hai.. doctors hai.. aur kitne saare... crores of engineers rahenge.. usme bhi unemployed hai... wo... kuch... life me ...* **Aap agar spiritual line me jaoge to sabse hatke alag se... aap karoge..**
(Everyone is getting educated now. There are engineers and doctors... and so many. crores of engineers will be there... among them, many are unemployed... they can't do much in life... But if you follow the spiritual path, you will be unique.)

Laaddo: *Ji...*
(Yes...)

Amol: **Wo jo life ka path hona chahiye, wo dusron se hatke hona chahiye...** *abhi wo revolution ka samay hai na.. Spiritual Revolution ka samay hai..*
(Your path in life should be unique and different from others. Now it is time for revolution... time for Spiritual Revolution.)

Laaddo:*Ji...*
(Yes...)

Amol: *Spiritual Revolution Shankar ke yug ka hai... Shankar kranti ke devta hai.. Hai na?*

(Spiritual Revolution belongs to the yuga of Shankar... Shankar is the deity of revolution... Right?)

Laaddo: *Ji...*
(Yes...)

Amol: *Wo abhi... aise samay... ye 5 years... 5-6 years... bahut important period hai... 2028 tak...*
(So now... at this time... these 5 years... These 5-6 years are a very crucial period... until 2028.)

Laaddo: *Ji...*
(Yes...)

Amol: *Abhi fast apko aage badhna hai.. speed se sabse aage jaana hai... Agar apki admission agar school me late hogaya to... apko peeche ka syllabus cover karna padta hai na...?*
(You must move forward quickly now... go ahead faster than everyone else... If you get admitted late to school, you must cover the earlier syllabus, right?)

Laaddo: *Ji...*
(Yes...)

Amol: *Waise hi... Aap agar abhi idhar aaye ho to Baba ke itne cassettes chale hai, itni murliyan chali hai.. apko to cover karna padega na saara knowledge...*
(Same way... Since you've come here now, so many cassettes have been played... so many Murlis (preachings) have been given... you'll need to cover all that knowledge, right?)

Laaddo: *Ji...*
(Yes...)

Amol: *Everything... to... uske liye to apko dusron se jyada mehnat karni padegi...*
(Everything... So, for that, you'll have to work harder than others.)

Laaddo: *Ji bhaiji...*
(Yes, bhaiji...)

Amol: *Baba ki murliyon me dher saare secrets hai...* apko samajhne padenge... Koi doubts aata hai to mereko pooch sakte ho... Hmm?
(There are many secrets in Baba's preachings... you'll have to understand them... If you have any questions, you can ask me,.. okay?)

Laaddo: Ji...
(Yes...)

Amol: *Phone kar sakte ho kabhi bhi... theek hai?... message daal deneka hai, jab bhi lagta hai baat karne ke liye...*
(You can call me any time... alright?... just drop a message whenever you feel like talking...)

Laaddo: *Ji bhaiji...*
(Okay bhaiji...)

Amol: *Koi bhi doubts hai, kuch bhi problem hai life me... kuch bhi hai.. aap mujhe batao.. theek hai?*
(Any doubts, any problems in life... anything at all... You tell me, okay?)

Laaddo:*Ji...*
(Yes...)

Amol: *Hesitate nahi karna hai...*
(Don't hesitate...)

Laaddo: *Ji...*
(Yes...)

The conversation shifted toward dismantling conventional aspirations. He told her that millions of engineers and doctors were unemployed, downplaying the value of education. He made it sound as though traditional career paths were insignificant in comparison to the "Spiritual Revolution" he was offering. He framed this movement as something grand and rare, making it seem like an exclusive opportunity that only a chosen few could be part of.

To reinforce this urgency, he emphasized that the next five to six years were crucial. "You have a lot to catch up on," he told her, comparing her situation to a student joining a class late and needing to cover the missed syllabus quickly. By doing so, he instilled a fear of being left behind, pushing her to invest more time and effort into their teachings. He encouraged her to study the Murlis, the cult's teachings, and keep copies of all available literature. "You can call me anytime if you have doubts," he reassured her, further solidifying himself as her guide.

Amol: *Aap jab bhatti karne aaoge, tab aap wapis aate aate Delhi hoke aana...*
(When you come for Bhatti, do go through Delhi while returning...)

Laaddo: *Ji...*
(Okay...)

Amol: Theek hai? Tabhi milenge aapse...
(Okay? Will meet you then...)

Laaddo: *Ji...*
(Okay...)

Amol: *Aur... waise... kab bhatti karne wale hain?*
(And... by the way... when are you going to undergo Bhatti?)

Laaddo: *October 2ⁿᵈ se chuttiyan chalu hogi tab karenge...*
(Holidays are going to begin from October 2nd... so I will do it then...)

Amol: *October 2ⁿᵈ se?*
(From October 2nd?)

Laaddo: *Ji...*
(Okay...)

Amol: *Lekin apka 18 years to 17 November ko ho raha hai na?*
(But you are completing 18 years of age on 17 November, right?)

Laaddo: *Agle saal 17 November ko ho raha hai, Bhaiji...*
(On 17ᵗʰ November of next year, Bhaiji...)

Amol: *Haan... wahi baat to mai bata raha tha Nisha Behen ko... wo bol rahi*

thi is saal ho raha hai karke... Aap... kya hai...? kaunsa year hai? Birth year?
(Yes... I was also telling the same thing to Nisha... But she was saying that you will complete 18 this year... What's your birth year?)

Laaddo: *2005...*
(2005...)

Amol: *2005... haan...* **18 years complete hoga apka 2023...** *Ok to aap Bhatti kar hi lo phir October ke baad...*
(2005... yes... you'll complete 18 years in 2023... Okay, then do the Bhatti after October for sure...)

He brought up the concept of Bhatti, a rigorous seven-day indoctrination program considered essential for complete surrender to their ideology. Conducted at their headquarters in Kampil, Farrukhabad, UP, the training is led by women who have already committed themselves fully to the doctrine. The purpose of Bhatti is deep psychological conditioning, ensuring that participants internalize the cult's beliefs unquestioningly. Upon completion, individuals are required to sign an affidavit, pledging absolute obedience to the group's prescribed norms. Any deviation from this pledge gives the cult the authority to take action against them, including exclusion from the group, something members are constantly reminded of.

He carefully noted her age, acknowledging that she was still under eighteen but would soon be eligible for deeper involvement.

Amol: *Bhatti hone ke baad dheere dheere apna seva mein involve ho jao... chota chota... abhi to kar hi rahi ho... aur bhi... aur seekho acche se... theek hai?*
(After Bhatti, start gradually involving yourself in service, small tasks. However, you're already doing a little of it as for now... keep learning more. Okay?)

Laaddo:*Ji Bhaiji...*
(Okay Bhaiji...)

Amol: *Aur... course karaana aana chahiye tumhe... Dheere dheere seekh jaogi... jab Bhatti karogi to achche se buddhi mein baith jaayega sab...*
(And... you should be able to teach the course to others. Gradually, you'll learn. Once you undergo Bhatti, everything will settle clearly in your mind...)

Laaddo: *Ji...*
(Okay...)

"Once you complete Bhatti, everything will fall into place," he assured her, conditioning her to see this training as the next milestone in her journey.

Secrecy was another crucial aspect of his manipulation.

Amol: *Apko... abhi to thoda sa gupt rehkar hi saara seva karna hai... Hmm?*
(As of now, you need to do the service secretly. Okay?)

Laaddo: *Ji...*
(Okay...)

Amol: *Hai na...? Yukti se... Yukti se chalna hai dheere dheere... Theek hai?*
(Right? Using Yukti (tactically)... You need to move slowly using a strategy.)

Laaddo: *Ji...*
(Okay...)

He emphasized the importance of *"Yukti"*, the use of strategy and tact, presenting secrecy as an intelligent and necessary approach. *"Move forward using Yukti,"* he advised, making it sound like a wise and calculated choice rather than a deceptive one. By framing it this way, he ensured that she would hide her growing involvement from those who might challenge or question it.

By the end of the call, Amol had successfully created a framework in which she was to see him as her mentor, the cult's teachings as her new purpose, and secrecy as her duty. He had subtly questioned her existing life, redefined success and ambition, and planted the idea that true fulfillment lay in complete devotion.

What seemed like an ordinary introductory conversation was a carefully structured psychological maneuver, an expertly laid foundation for the deeper control that was yet to come.

I was stunned when I finally grasped the depth of their psychological trap, the intricate web they had slowly woven around my Laaddo. Everything became clear when I heard the recordings of their calls and observed how cleverly they manipulated her innocence. Every word, every pause, every layer of emotional influence suddenly made sense. All the missing pieces came together in that moment, and they painted a terrifying picture of systematic control.

This was no ordinary spiritual path they were leading her into. It was a planned system of indoctrination, reinforced with rituals like the Bhatti, designed to strip away logic, emotion, and family ties.

(**Note:** *The conversations and reflections shared in this section are drawn from my personal experience as a mother, navigating an unimaginable situation. I have not conducted any technical or forensic analysis, but like any attentive parent, I've listened deeply, not just to the words, but to the silences, the tone, the shifts in energy. What I've shared is not a verdict, but my perception, a mother's instinct, heart, and truth. Readers may interpret things differently, and I respect that. If you notice any insights I might have missed or if you find a perspective that portrays Amol's actions in a different or more positive light, I genuinely welcome your feedback. This book is not just a testimony; it is a search for understanding, healing, and truth.*)

****

CHAPTER VII

Surrendered Before She Knew

43

Cult leaders don't shout; they whisper. And those whispers turn into the loudest truths for innocent minds.

Before my daughter ever stepped foot in Delhi, a subtle yet strategic grooming process had already begun. The woman in charge of the so-called ashram, who projected herself as a spiritual guardian, was deliberately weaving a net of emotional and mental manipulation around her.

She would frequently send photos of the ashram's ambiance: cozy communal spaces, and serene faces locked in meditative silence. But these weren't just ordinary photos; each one was carefully chosen or even clicked by Amol himself, crafted to sell a dream, not reflect the truth.

The lady would ask Laaddo, "*Which photo do you like the most and why?*" This seemingly innocent question was not just about her preference; it was a psychological entry point, an invitation to emotionally invest. It made my Laaddo reflect, imagine, and begin attaching her desires to a place she had never even seen. She was being gently encouraged to envision herself there, as if it were already meant for her.

Behind these innocent-looking exchanges was a much darker intent: to stir her curiosity, slowly detach her from her current reality, and get her to romanticize a life that promised purity, purpose, and peace... but would eventually isolate her from her family and identity.

Simultaneously, the pressure to gain my permission for her visit to Delhi was building. Every conversation at home was becoming a calculated push. She would bring it up often, sometimes casually, sometimes emotionally, trying to convince me that this trip would be a harmless spiritual experience, just a few days to find some mental peace. But I now see how that wasn't her voice alone speaking; it was the voice of that cult echoing through her. She had unknowingly become a channel, a bridge they were using to pull her away from me and deeper into their world.

In April 2023, after the completion of her 12th board exams, she again insisted that she wanted to visit the Delhi Ashram for a few days. She promised me that she would not do anything I disapproved of if I allowed her to go. Wanting to ensure her safety, I first confirmed with my cousin about the place and the people she intended to visit. My cousin assured me that she was going to the safest place and that I need not worry about her. Trusting both my daughter's and my cousin's assurance, I reluctantly permitted her, believing that she wanted to interact with spiritual-minded people and learn something valuable.

She stayed at their place in Delhi from April 29, 2023, to June 7, 2023. The woman who accompanied her on her journeys to and from Delhi was the one who **took my Laaddo away** on 1st December 2023. My daughter stayed there along with two other girls whose parents also believed in their ideology.

After she reached Delhi, our communication drastically reduced. She would call me only once a day, just as a formality. Whenever I reached out, she would claim she was too busy learning new things and hardly used her phone. Her engagement with them became so deep that she neglected important matters, including the college interviews for her admission. As a result, she missed the opportunity to secure admission into a reputed college.

During the summer vacation, my parents and sisters visited our home and longed to see her. However, she was not even willing to speak to them. Concerned about her distance from family and her missed college admission, I decided to call her back home after about a month of her stay. When I conveyed this to her, she made me speak to the person in charge over the phone. Back then, I had no negative feelings toward those people, believing them to be spiritual. Even I spoke to that in-charge lady with warmth, unaware that they were strategically collecting evidence to prove that I had willingly sent Laaddo to them. Later, to my surprise, I discovered the recording of that very call in her WhatsApp.

This was the first time Laaddo met Amol in person. He would visit the so-called ashram now and then, not as a distant figure, but as someone who blended in casually, yet always remained at the center of attention. Vidcos from those days, recorded in an unassuming manner, show glimpses of their interactions, simple on the surface, but deeply telling when seen with open eyes.

In one such video, Amol made a dramatic statement. With a casual laugh and a sense of false devotion in his tone, he declared, *"Agar Baba kahen, toh mai chauthi manzil se kood jaaun!"* (If Baba told me to, I'd jump from the fourth floor!).

It might sound like a lighthearted exaggeration to someone unfamiliar, but for the young, impressionable minds around him, girls like my Laaddo, it was a subtle lesson in loyalty.

He wasn't just expressing his devotion to a guru. He was planting an unspoken expectation: *"This is what surrender looks like. This is what you're expected to become."* No questions, no hesitation. Just blind faith, dressed in admiration and sacrifice.

Amol had mastered the art of appearing emotionally available, playful even, especially with the younger girls. He would casually sing Bollywood songs, popular romantic or soulful melodies, to create an aura of friendliness and warmth. He wasn't loud or forceful. That's what made it so dangerous. His charm didn't raise any immediate red flags. It was the quiet kind, the one that seeps into the heart without warning.

For my Laaddo, it must have felt like a space where emotions, spirituality, and admiration all blended. A man who claimed such extreme devotion could easily convince others to follow him the same way. Slowly, unknowingly, he became the model of trust and surrender for the girls.

And in that environment, wrapped in poetry, songs, laughter, and exaggerated tales of loyalty, my Laaddo was being taught a new definition of devotion, one that didn't include parents, one that asked her to cut ties with those who truly loved her, so she could merge completely into the identity they were shaping for her. These weren't just random interactions. These were rehearsed layers of influence, carefully tailored to mold innocent hearts.

After returning home, my daughter was physically present but emotionally absent. Whenever she spent a little time with me, all she talked about was those people. Most of the time, she remained occupied with them, either talking to them or carrying out tasks assigned by them. I expressed my concerns, sometimes in sadness and sometimes with frustration, telling her that I missed her despite her being right there. However, instead of reassuring me, she would report everything to them.

On their advice, she even started recording our conversations. I later found several **voice recordings where I was counselling her**, explaining to her the true meaning of sewa (selfless service). In one of those recordings, I sarcastically remarked that I saw her surrendering herself to them. Although I regretted saying it immediately, she took those words seriously and, unfortunately, she had already recorded them.

Her every step, every reaction, was guided by Amol. He was coaching her on how to handle me, ensuring that she remained firmly in his grasp while distancing herself further from me.

One of the voice recordings I later discovered in her WhatsApp chats exposed the disturbing depth of Amol's psychological grip on my daughter. It was from the time she had visited Delhi and was sitting with the group (Amol, Nisha, and one more girl). As per their usual practice, the conversation was deliberately recorded so they could revisit it later to clarify their doubts. But what struck me was how methodical Amol's approach was; he never issued direct commands. Instead, he carefully planted doubts, fears, and a false sense of divine duty, skillfully shaping her thoughts to align with their ideology. It wasn't a conversation but was indoctrination disguised as guidance. The way he subtly reinforced his influence left no room for independent thinking. It was all a part of their manipulative process, designed to erase her inner voice and replace it with theirs.

Summary of the Conversation, including some Key Dialogues:

- Amol dismissed those who had ever questioned or chosen to leave the group, branding them as weak and incapable of true surrender. According to him, such people never truly belonged in the first place, and their departure was inevitable. He made it seem as if staying was not just an act of faith but a testament to one's strength, subtly instilling in my daughter the fear that even considering an exit meant failure.
- He reinforced this fear with apocalyptic predictions, claiming that by 2028, all who followed Ashtadev would eventually return to Baba (VDD). He spoke of planctary collisions and cosmic disasters, painting a grim picture of the world outside the cult. This fear-based control mechanism ensured that my daughter saw no future beyond their ideology. When questioned about VDD's whereabouts, Amol did not deny that he was in hiding. Instead, he justified it, presenting VDD as a divine figure unfairly persecuted by the world. He insisted that true followers had a duty to protect Baba at all costs, reinforcing secrecy as a virtue.

A few of their real-time conversations are as follows:

Amol: 23 me uske(Ashtadev ke) jo baramanke hai, unke baramanke ke buddhi me aane lagega ki humara part hai iss panchve number ke purvaj ke saath janm janmantar ka... unke buddhi me yeh baatein baitthne lagegi...
(During the year 2023, his twelve selected souls will begin to realize in their minds that they have a role with the fifth-numbered ancestor across many lifetimes... this thought will start settling into their consciousness...)

Girl: *23 me kaun? Barah kaun?*
(Who in 2023? Who are those twelve gems?)

Amol:*Hmm... 23 ke December tak unki buddhi me yeh batein betthne lagegi... aur 28-29 tak jake wo apni seat pe set ho jayengi... aur seva sab se jyada karke dikhayenge... sirf baitthne ki baat nahi hai, sankalpon me samjho 25 ke baitth gaya, lekin usme se jo barah 28-29 tak sewa ka stock... itna unko sahyog denge... itna seva ka stock jama karenge din raat... woh actual me barah me set ho jayenge apni seat pe...*
(By December 2023, these thoughts will begin to settle into their minds... and by the years 2028–29, they will firmly take their seats... and will prove themselves by offering the maximum service. It's not just about taking a seat mentally, say 25 of them realize their connection, but among them, the twelve who accumulate immense service, who tirelessly gather the stock of service day and night... only those will truly be fixed in their seat among the twelve gems.)

Girl:*To abhi se pata chal raha hai unko?*
(So, have they already started realizing it?)

Amol:*Unko abhi sankalp ho gaya hai... aaraha hai unke...*
(They have now made the determination... they are feeling it within...)

Girl:*Unko aana hai paanchve number ke poorvaj ko ye pata chal raha hai ke ye aa sakte hai?*
(Is the fifth-numbered ancestor realizing who among them is getting selected as the twelve gems?)

Amol:*Paanchve number ke purvaj ko toh.... dheere dheere pata chal raha hai... aur uski janm janmantar ki connection wali aatmayein... abhi jo jithna sachchai se uske prati arpan me hongi...*
(The fifth-numbered ancestor is slowly beginning to understand... and those souls connected to him across lifetimes... it depends on how sincerely they surrender to him now...)

When one of the girls questioned their role, to further reinforce the idea of unwavering commitment, he repeatedly emphasized that true surrender could only be considered valid after a person turned 18. Yet, the conditioning started much earlier, strategically grooming young minds to perceive that eventual surrender as not just desirable, but inevitable.

Amol often spoke about a chosen group, the top twelve followers, whom he referred to as Barah Manke, who would come to realize their divine roles by the end of 2023 and begin proving themselves through relentless service. He positioned himself as the "fifth-numbered ancestor," claiming to be one of the Ashtadevs, which added a mythological authority to his words.

This timeline was no coincidence. My daughter was set to turn 18 in November 2023. By stressing the importance of December 2023, he ensured that she would be mentally and emotionally prepared for deeper immersion in their ideology at just the right moment.

If she wished to be counted among the twelve, the message was clear: she needed to act before the end of 2023. This narrative of exclusivity and competition, of needing to prove one's devotion before others claimed those sacred spots, was a calculated strategy to push her further into submission.

*****

Nisha:_Inko(to Laaddo) samjhaiye Bhaiji, late aane se thodi kuch hota hai..._
(Bhaiji, explain to her(Laaddo) that she is not yet late...)

Amol(to Laaddo): _Purva janam ka aapko pata thodi hai... Aapko pata thodi hai aap kithne nazdik the aur aapne kya part bajaya... Aise hi thodi hota hai... Koi jaldi aane wale chod ke bhaag jate hain... Sambandh jodna badi baat nahi hai... Sambandh anth tak nibhana badi baat hai... Sambandh toh sabhi jod lete hain... Pur anth tak nibhane wale bachte hain..._
(You don't know about your past birth, how close you were, and what role you played... It doesn't work like that... Some who come early, leave and run away... Making a connection is not a big thing... What matters is carrying that connection till the very end... Everyone can form relationships, but very few stay till the end...)

In this conversation, Nisha was asking Amol to explain to Laaddo that she wasn't late in joining. Amol, as always, diverted the focus towards past births, suggesting that she had played an important role in a previous life and was always spiritually close. He used this to assure her that coming late doesn't matter, what matters is staying till the end. Through this, he subtly reinforced the idea that forming a bond with the group is easy, but true value lies in staying committed, planting the thought that leaving now would mean she lacks depth or faith. This was another way of manipulating her emotions and keeping her hooked.

*****

Nisha: *Potamail me kya likhna chahiye bhaiji? bataiye...*
(What are the things to be written in Potamail Bhaiji? Please tell...)

Amol:*Potamail me mukhya galti toh kaam vikaar se related hai... Apni awastha... Apne mann me vikrut sankalp aate hi hai. Kiske prati aate hai. Saari baatein deni chahiye. Aur, apni awastha, apna seva... kaise chal raha hai... Kisike prati irsha dvesh ke sankalp, woh toh nahi aa rahe... Buddhi bahar ki duniya me toh nahi bhaag rahi hai.*
(Prominently, Potamail is all about lustful feelings for someone... Your situation... You will be getting those lustful feelings... For whom... All those things to be mentioned... Your sewa-related details... If you have any hatred for anyone... If your mind is running behind the outside world.

Nisha: *Ji...*
(Okay...)

Amol: *Mukhya hai Amrutvela... Amrutvela theek se kar rahe hain ya nahi? Koi koi ko sewayen soumpi jaati hai, aur woh dikhane ke liye sewa leke baitth jate hain, aur do do mahina kuch sewa hi nahi karte... aur baba ko report hi nahi milti hai, ki yeh sewaayen toh humne di thi, aur koi yeh aage hi nahi badhi... Aur sachchai se batate hi nahi hai. Apne paas sewayen leke baith jate hai. Woh bhi sachchai se likhna chahiye, mujhe yeh sewayen di gayi thi, lekin maine aaj tak yeh kiya hi nahi hai. Meri tabiyat theek nahi thi... mai aage se karungi... maine albelapan kiya... maine alasya kiya... aage se mai karungi... sachchai honi chahiye har baat me...*
(If you are following Amrutvela timings properly or not.. Some were given some responsibilities, and they simply sat without doing any service for about 2 months or more... And Baba doesn't get any report of it, that he has given the responsibilities which are not fulfilled... Those things also should be written sincerely... That I was given these responsibilities, and I couldn't fulfil them as I was lazy.. Will do it honestly hereafter... Honesty should always be there.)

Control within the group extended beyond ideology into strict surveillance. Amol spoke about Potamail letters, followers were required to write, detailing their daily spiritual service and confessing their impure thoughts. This system not only ensured compliance but also created a sense of guilt, making members feel constantly watched and evaluated.

*****

Laaddo: *Abhi barah ho jayenge fir jo 13th rahega uska kya part rahega?*
(Now, after those first 12, what will be the role of the 13th one?)

Amol: *Kya part rahega? woh toh raj parivar ka bhaagi hai... Jo pehle barah hai woh...*
(What would be the role? He will be part of the royal family... In the royal family of the first 12.)

Laaddo: *Nahi toh... Wo mala me to nahi aayega na lekin?*
(But they will not be counted among those 12 gems... right?)

Amol: *Arey woh 108 ki mala me nahi aayega, lekin jo 108 mala ke manke unke subordinate hands me hai na woh... jaise aatth (8) ashtadev, barah barah ko tayyar karega... barah aur uske neeche ke logon ko tayyar karenge... toh... woh subordinate hands me hai... aur uske baad... woh bhi prince princess banenge... Raj parivar me janam lenge...*
(Even though they don't come under those first 108, they will be counted under the subordinate hands of those 108.. Like... 8 Ashtadev will prepare 12 gems under each of them... And so they will be under those subordinate hands, and later they will become a Prince or Princess... Will take birth in royal families.)

Laaddo: *Toh slight... 12th aur 13th me slight differences se woh mala me nahi aake aur uske andar ke group me aayenge...aise?*
(So, because of the slight difference between 12th and 13th, they come under their subordinate groups instead of the main mala. Is that it?)

Amol: *Haan... Parivaar me toh aayega na... Raj parivar toh bada rehta hai na... toh sabka lakshya Raja bann ne ka thodi hai? Koi Rani bhi bann na chahta hai... Koi Patrani bhi bann na chahta hai...*
(Yes... But they come under the royal family... Right? The royal family is large, and so everyone doesn't aim to become king... Some want to become a princess... Some want to become the queen...)

When my daughter asked about the 13th follower, it reflected her concern about not being among the top 12. Amol's vague response kept her hopeful yet uncertain, subtly encouraging her to strive harder for validation and a higher spiritual rank. This ambiguity was a tactic to keep followers emotionally invested and constantly proving their worth.

*****

Amol: *Ashtadev apas me takra takra ke jab alag ho jate, toh unke number declare ho jate hai... Jhagda toh bada jhagda 18 (2018) ke ending me hi hua ...* **Aur mai meri seat pe set hogaya.**
(When the Ashtadevs clash and separate, their ranks get declared... The major conflict happened at the end of 2018... **and I secured my seat.**)

He indicated that he is one of the Ashtadevs. This statement reinforced his authority and position within the cult's hierarchy, making his influence over the followers even stronger.

When one of the girls asked about the prediction of their future life partners...

Girl: *Toh jo humare partner honge, woh BK me honge. Toh...*
(So would our partner be in BK?)

Amol: *Yahan bhi honge... jo jo jodiyan yahan bhi hogi, jo Ashtadev part dhari hai.... hain na... Jaise baap hai, toh waise* **baap ke prati jab arpan hogaye, toh kanyaein kya hogayi uski, patni bangayi ya nahi bangayi?**
Abhi jo kanyaein hai, yagya me. Unka baba ke saath connection juta ya nahi juta? Sambandh juta ya nahi juta? Juta... Toh Dwaparyug me raaniyan bann sakti hai ki nai bann sakti hai. Jagdamba Baba ki rani banti hai ya nahi banti hai... 63 janmon me raaj parivar me aake rani bhi banegi. Lekin jo 21 janam hai, woh jodidaar Vijaymala(BKs) me hai. Samajh raha hai kya? Satyug-Tretayug ka jo 21 janam ka jodidaar hai, woh vijaymala me hai. Lekin jo Dwaparyug se leke Kaliyug tak jo janam hai, dher sare, 63 janam liye hai, uska shooting yaha hoga ya nahi hoga? Yaha hoga.
Waise hi yaha Rudhramala(AIVV) ke andar, jo partner bane hue hai, woh oonch part dhari hoga ya koi aira gaira nathu khaira hoga? *Kisiko koi bhi partner bann jayega?*
(They might be here also... the couples formed here, those who are playing the role of Ashtadev, and the virgin girls who surrendered themselves to the father, then what would be the relation between them? Wouldn't she be his wife?

Now, the virgin girls in the yagya had relations with Baba or not? They had...so...would they become queens in Dwaparyug or not? Would Jagdamba become queen of Baba or not? In all 63 births, she will be the queen of the royal family. But in the remaining 21 births, her partner will be in Vijayamala.. Are you following what I'm saying? The partner of 21 births of Satyuga and Tretayuga will be in Vijayamala... but for the 63 births of Dwapar and Kalyuga, the shooting period is going on here now...

In the same way... in this Rudramala(AIVV), would the ones who have become partners be of the higher post or any useless person? Can any useless person become a partner?)

Girl: *Oonch part dhari hoga.*
(He will be in a higher post...)

Amol: *Oonch part dhari hoga... **Jo part dhaari apne seat pe set hai, usi part dhaari ke saath jodi banane ki abhilasha rahegi?** Ya jo apne seat pe set nahi hai, kal jaake bhag jayega... uske andar... woh thodi jodi banega? Jo seat pe set hai, toh jitni kanyaein aaj ki date me, Baba jab tak the yagya me, woh unko arpan hoti thi. Jaise Jagdamba hai... uski Baba ke saath jodi bann gayi. Usme dikhate hai 16,108 ke saath raas... yeh karte hue, raas rachate hue.*
(**A girl would naturally wish to be paired with someone who is firmly seated in his destined role.** But what about the one who is unsettled and might leave tomorrow? How can he be considered a true partner? Those who are firmly in their roles, just as in earlier times when Baba was present in the Yagya, were claimed by him. Just like Jagdamba, who was united with Baba. It is depicted that he performed Raas (divine dance) with 16,108 souls, engaging in this sacred act.)

His words carried a sinister implication. Amol subtly influenced the girls' thoughts, making them believe that they should seek a partner who was deeply committed to this ideology. By framing it this way, he indirectly positioned himself as their ideal partner, following VDD's footsteps. VDD treated virgin girls as his wives, engaging in physical relations with them, and that Amol was merely following in his footsteps.

*****

Laaddo: *Abhi jo aapka part hai, usko bahar kaise samjhayenge?*
(How will you explain your role to the outside world?)
Amol: *Bahar toh kya samjhayenge?*
(Why would I explain it to the outside world..)

Laaddo: *Bahar, matlab...Gyan ki duniya me..*
(Outside world.. I mean.. Among PBKs..)

Amol:*PBK ke andar ke log samajh nahi pate hai... bahar ke duniya wale thodi samjhenge?*
(PBKs themselves don't understand.. How would the people in the outer world understand?)

Laaddo: *PBKs me kaise samjhayenge?*
(How would you explain it to PBKs?)

Amol: PBKs me toh... Baba ne bola hai 18 [2018] me aath (8) set ho jate hai apne part ke upar... *2018 me aath (8) ko pata chal jayega ki mera mala me number kya hai... Baba ne bola seva ke aadhar pe hi pata chalta hai...Unhone jo Ishwariya seva kiye hai... Uss sewa ke aadhar se number bante hai... Ashtadev alag alag departments ke head honge... Yagya me alag alag department hai...*
(Baba has already told PBKs that in 2018, all 8 (ashtadevs) will be settled in their roles.. All 8 of them will know their position in 2018.. Baba told that based on sewa only, everyone will know.. Their place will be fixed based on the Godly sewa they do.. Ashtadevs will be the heads of different departments.. There are different departments in this yagya..)

In this conversation, Laaddo asks Amol how he would explain his role as an Ashtadev to others, especially within the PBK community. Amol dismisses the idea of explaining it to the outside world, claiming even PBKs themselves cannot understand. He refers to a 2018 prophecy by "Baba" that eight souls (Ashtadevs) would recognize their roles based on the Godly service they perform, with each heading different departments within the Yagya. Through vague spiritual justifications and references to divine authority, Amol subtly positions himself as one of these chosen leaders, avoiding direct answers and reinforcing the cult's closed and hierarchical belief system.

*****

Amol: *Jo 18 saal se chote hai, unka toh koi surrender ka yeh nahi hai.* **18 saal se jo bade hain, unki buddhi mature ho gayi hai. Abhi agar woh surrender hote hain, soch samajh ke. To unko fir, yeh karna hai, lekin jab Baba yagya me nahi hai, Ashtdev me se kisi bhi ek Ashtadev ka paala pakad rahe hain, to bhi baap ka hi paala hai na. Kal jake, woh Ashtadev jithne bhi parivar tayyar karega, wo baap ko hi soumpega na.. 28 [2028] tak aate aate..**
(The ones who are below 18 years, their surrender is not considered. **But the ones who are above 18 years, their minds are mature enough, and if**

they get themselves surrendered, then they have to do. But now, when Baba is not present, he said, if you follow any of the Ashtadevs, it means that you are following Baba only. In the future, that is, by the end of 2028, those Ashtadevs will hand over all the families created by them to Baba only.)

The reference to VDD's "return" suggested that these young girls were merely being held in waiting until they could be handed over to him. My Laaddo, in her innocence, failed to grasp the disturbing undertones of his words. She took everything at face value, believing in their so-called spiritual purity without realizing the deeper, darker meaning behind them.

*****

Amol:*Yeh to mera extra ordinary janam hai... mera pichla janam to 84 hai.... Usme Paramanand Kundanmal tha mai... Paramanand Kundanmal, Om Mandali ka vakeel... Dekha hai kya usko? Yagya ke aadi me Om Mandali ka vakeel tha... Yagya ke aadi me jab, 1937 se leke cases hona chalu hogaye... 1937-38 me... Uss samay saare cases Paramanand Kundanmal ne ladhe the... Baba ne bola, aadi so anth... 17-18 (2017-18) me firse cases ho gaye... Woh saare cases firse usi Paramanand Kundanmal ne ladhe, 17-18 me...* **Aur dekhne me woh kithna Hero dikhta hai..Parmanand Kundanmal... Dekho kya personality hai... Uss samay ka famous vakeel tha, bohot romantic vyakti tha...**

(This is my extraordinary birth... My last birth was my 84th... In that, I was Paramanand Kundanmal... Paramanand Kundanmal, the lawyer of Om Mandali... Have you seen him? At the beginning of the Yagya, he was Om Mandali's lawyer... When the court cases started around the beginning of the Yagya, around the year 1937-38, all those cases were fought by Paramanand Kundanmal... Baba had said, "As the beginning, so the end"... In 2017-18, again, the cases happened... And again, those cases were fought by the same Paramanand Kundanmal in 2017-18... **And just look at how much of a hero he looks like... Paramanand Kundanmal... Just look at that personality... He was a famous lawyer of that time, and a very romantic person...**)

Amol also highlighted that he was Parmanand Kundanmal, who was an Advocate of Dada Lekhraj, founder of Bhramakumaris, linking himself to an important historical figure within their belief system. Amol also declared that this was his extraordinary birth after completing 84 births, positioning himself as a divine being with a predetermined role in this so-called spiritual mission.

*****

There's one moment captured in the recording: a conversation so ordinary on the surface, yet so piercing when heard with a mother's heart. Nisha's phone rings. It's her father.

Nisha: *Bhaiji... Papa ka phone hai... uthau kya?*
(Bhaiji... It's Papa's call... should I answer it?)

She doesn't jump to answer. She doesn't smile at the sound of her father's name. She pauses, not because she's unsure what to say to him, but because she's unsure whether she should. The daughter who once used to run to the phone when her father called, now looked toward someone else, Amol, for permission.

And Amol? His reply wasn't even a direct answer.

Amol: *Kyu? Karna kya hai? Huh?*
(Why? What is he going to do? Huh?)

As if a father calling his daughter was suspicious. As if love from home needed justification.

In that moment, it wasn't just about answering a phone. It was about how deeply she had been conditioned. Nisha wasn't showing eagerness to speak with her father. She didn't even want to. But because Amol was sitting there, watching, she asked. And when he chose to dismiss the question and not give a direct response, she moved slightly away from the group, only then did she reluctantly answer the call.

After the call ended, she laughed as she told Amol what her father had asked.

Nisha: *Mere pitaji address puch rahe the... koi problem toh nahi hai na... kuch chahiye kya...*
(My father was asking for the address... there's no problem, right? Do you need anything?)

While her father sat miles away, worried sick, longing to hear her voice, desperately hoping that maybe, just maybe, his daughter would say she missed him too.

But she didn't. Because the daughter he loved was no longer fully there. Her words, her tone, her laugh; they weren't coming from the child he

56

raised, but from the layers of conditioning placed above her heart.

The pain in this moment wasn't loud. It was quiet, almost invisible to an outsider. But to a parent who knows what love sounds like, what real connection feels like, it was shattering. That phone call wasn't just a conversation; it reflected how far she had been pulled away from the people who truly cared.

That's how control works. It isn't always visible in chains or rules. Sometimes, it hides in silence. In laughter at the wrong moment. In hesitation before picking up a phone. In seeking permission to love one's own family.

My Laaddo, caught in this web of manipulation, was slowly being conditioned to see questioning as betrayal and obedience as enlightenment. The conversation reflected her internal conflict; her mind struggling to grasp these doctrines while her heart sought validation from Amol. The more she listened, the deeper she was pulled in, unknowingly surrendering pieces of herself to an illusion that was tightening its grip with every passing moment.

My Laaddo's journey into their group was not a sudden leap but a gradual entrapment, cleverly disguised as a privilege. They gave her tasks that made her feel valued and indispensable; editing and uploading videos of VDD, designing banners for seminars led by Amol in schools and colleges, and later managing their YouTube channel titled "*Spiritual revolution*," where they upload the recordings of those seminars after editing. These responsibilities were portrayed as special assignments, reserved only for the most "*chosen*" ones. She was made to feel like a vital part of their so-called core team, essential to their mission, their cause, their movement.

One of the most disturbing strategies they used was the systematic erasure of real identities. My Laaddo, like all others, was made to change her name frequently during online sessions, hiding her true self. They were also instructed to create multiple email accounts, further fracturing any sense of personal authenticity. When I once asked her the reason behind this bizarre name-changing ritual, she casually replied, "*The outside world is too bad, Maa. We have to hide who we really are.*" I laughed it off at the time, thinking it was a childish fantasy, something harmless.

I had no idea then that this was the beginning of a deep psychological manipulation, one that would slowly blur the lines between her identity and theirs. The group addressed each other using their newly assigned names, only to change them again just days later. At that time, I didn't even know what a cult was, or that someone could be brainwashed into joining one.

But what initially seemed like a privilege soon turned into a burden. Deadlines were imposed, and she was indirectly accused of lacking commitment when she failed to meet them. Without realizing it, she **began surrendering to their instructions, sacrificing her health, food, sleep, and studies.** Amol demanded that she submit her seva report daily, ensuring that she completed her work at any cost. Mistakes were met with scolding, while occasional praise kept her desperate for validation. The emotional push-and-pull strategy was clear. In one moment, he would make her feel special, and in the next, he would withhold his attention, creating a deep emotional dependency. It was a psychological game designed to break her self-worth and make her feel she had to constantly prove herself to earn his validation.

One particular message Laaddo wrote to Amol on **July 7, 2023,** a few days after returning from Delhi, speaks volumes about the mental and emotional turmoil she was going through:

(Translated Version of the Letter)

> "*Bhaiji.... I have been wanting to tell you something for several days now, but I didn't have the courage because I didn't know how you would take it.*
>
> *I have just recently come into this knowledge. Based on what little I have understood since joining this group, I have been doing seva, creating clips, writing titles, and editing videos. Many times,*

I don't fully grasp the points, and even when I do, I get confused about the titles. I also make mistakes.

You expect a lot from me, but I still need to understand more. I have only just entered this path, Bhaiji. I don't have as much knowledge as Nisha Di or Shivani Di. Since joining, I have been focusing more on Seva. I haven't even completed my course yet, Bhaiji.

I did not come here fully prepared; you will have to shape me so that I can serve better.

Your expectations are valid, and I genuinely try to meet them. I want to do more seva, but I realize I make mistakes. I don't know what to do. Please guide me.

Many times, I look forward to your reply. I have also noticed that you respond to others but not to me. I have seen it with my own eyes. I am not bringing this up to say that I have a problem, because then you might feel I am complaining. I don't have any issue with whom you talk to, but when I ask for something related to Seva, please reply so that I can proceed with my work and complete it on time.

But I keep waiting for you. At night, I stay up obsessed over my work while my mother scolds me for not sleeping. She waits for me to sleep, but I argue with her because you told me this work needs to be completed urgently. For example, you wanted a video to be made public by morning, so I spent two days seriously working on it, but you didn't even check it in time. Even when I ask something about Seva, you don't respond, and that makes me afraid to ask about anything else.

I don't mind if you scold me for my mistakes, but please understand my problems too, Bhaiji. I am sharing them with you so that you can help me solve them.

I feel like I don't know what is right or wrong anymore. I don't understand what is going on in your mind.

It seems like you don't respond properly to me, yet you expect a lot. I try my best, using whatever intelligence I have, even if I don't fully understand things. I spend all day learning and trying to complete my tasks despite restrictions. I even tolerate the taunts of others, but I still feel like you are ignoring me.

I don't know why, but I feel like my efforts are being ignored. I am not waiting for credit or appreciation. I don't expect you to acknowledge me, but I just want to know, am I doing my seva properly? That's all I am thinking about. Since I joined late and don't have as much knowledge as others, if you have expectations of me, then you should also train me accordingly so that I can improve my seva.

There were many times I felt hurt.

I tried to tell you before, but I couldn't. Even when I was there in person, I saw you ignoring me while talking to others. I kept waiting, thinking you would reply so that I could continue my seva in the right direction, but you wouldn't respond on time, and that hurt me a lot. Yet, you expected me to complete Seva immediately. I am here because I am connected to you. After all, I want to do seva, and because I am connected to Baba. I do whatever I understand, and if I don't understand something, I ask others. Sorry, Bhaiji, but I feel like you are being partial.

SORRY if I have hurt you. ”

Tears streamed down my face as I realized how oblivious I had been to the depths of manipulation my Laaddo was enduring. The weight of my ignorance crushed me, knowing that while I trusted her words, she was silently struggling under the pressure of impossible expectations. She was trapped in a cycle of emotional control, her self-worth dictated by validation that was deliberately withheld. This was not spirituality; this was control in its most insidious form. And it was only getting worse.

(**Note:** *The conversations and reflections shared in this section are drawn from my personal experience as a mother navigating an unimaginable situation. I have not conducted any technical or forensic analysis, but like any attentive parent, I've listened deeply, not just to the words, but to the silences, the tone, the shifts in energy. What I've shared is not a verdict, but my perception, a mother's instinct, heart, and truth. Readers may interpret things differently, and I respect that. If you notice any insights I might have missed or if you find a perspective that portrays Amol's actions in a different or more positive light, I genuinely welcome your feedback. This book is not just a testimony; it is a search for understanding, healing, and truth.*)

****

CHAPTER VIII

Confrontations in Court

The burden of proof is on the victim, but how do you prove coercion when the victim has been conditioned to defend their abuser?

The moment I realized my Laaddo had been ensnared by the cult, I decided to take drastic steps to bring her back, not just physically, but emotionally and mentally. On **January 18, 2024,** after tirelessly gathering evidence, I filed a Writ Petition in the Delhi High Court.

My heart weighed heavily as I embarked on this difficult legal journey, but I had no other choice. Fighting for my Laaddo's freedom meant standing against her will in a courtroom, a place that was as unfamiliar to me as it was to her. The thought of confronting her in such a setting filled me with anguish, yet it was a step I had to take.

I couldn't help but recall how she used to hold my hand tightly whenever she felt insecure, whether during a doctor's visit or in any situation that made her uncomfortable. Her small, firm grip was her silent plea for reassurance, and I was always there to give it.

But now, as I prepared to face her in court, the roles were reversed. I found myself wondering, "*Who will hold her hand when she feels afraid in the courtroom?*"

The thought ripped through me, leaving a hollow ache. Despite everything, I knew she needed comfort even if she couldn't or wouldn't turn to me for it anymore.

The courtroom wasn't just a place for legal arguments; it was a battlefield for our emotions.

I could only hope that the love we once shared would somehow reach her, even across the courtroom divide.

At this point, I must acknowledge the strength God bestowed upon me. I believe it was His unseen hand that kept me standing firm when everything around me was shaking.

My daughter was being manipulated, and the only way I could save her was to challenge the system that had taken her away from me. As I submitted my case, I could only pray that the evidence I had painstakingly collected would be enough to make the court see the truth.

The case was initially heard by a Single Bench, but as the names AIVV and VDD had already been noticed by the court in previous cases, the cult's influence over my daughter became more apparent, and the gravity of the situation was felt. So, it was transferred to a Double Bench and eventually reached the Chief Justice himself.

The legal battle was only just beginning, but the emotional toll it took on me was immeasurable.

The first time my daughter appeared in court, she was escorted by two cult followers, one of whom was Nisha, along with the police, ostensibly for her protection from me. She had been made to wear a saree, a symbolic gesture by the cult to make her feel like an adult, as though age and appearance were sufficient markers of maturity. But she looked distant, as if she were no longer the same girl who had once held my hand, laughing and living life with joy.

Her expression was cold, her movements mechanical, and she avoided my gaze entirely. When the judge asked her if she wanted to speak to me, her refusal was sharp and unfeeling.

"I have nothing to speak to her," she said, her voice devoid of the warmth I once knew.

*****

On the day of the second hearing before the Double Bench, my counsel requested that she be placed in a neutral environment, somewhere free from the cult's influence, where she could think independently.

Immediately, my daughter intervened.

"I am a major now," she declared firmly.

"Not even the court can send me anywhere without my approval."

Her words reflected not just her newfound sense of autonomy but also the legal loopholes that had been carefully explained to her by Amol. It wasn't merely the cult's broad teachings at work; it was a deliberate manipulation of the law, instilled in her to shield the cult's control under the guise of personal freedom.

It was heartbreaking to see her insist on her adulthood, unaware that she was merely parroting the beliefs fed to her. The cult hadn't just conditioned her mind; it had taken full control of her spirit, her will, and her very sense of self.

During the hearing on **January 22, 2024,** an order was passed instructing the **SDM** and **DCP** of Southwest Delhi to inspect their premises. However, this turned out to be futile; they found no evidence of manipulation. It wasn't surprising. The manipulation wasn't physical but psychological and emotional.

All the inmates submitted written statements willingly, expressing their desire to stay.

The inspection report, which was submitted on **January 24,** leaned heavily in favor of the so-called ashram.

The court process was painfully slow, making it feel like the truth might never fully come to light. The case moved before the Chief Justice. After hearing, he sensed that something deeper was wrong. Slowly, he started grasping the extent of the cult's psychological control.

On **January 31, 2024,** during the next hearing, the Chief Justice, recognizing the need for sensitivity, called my daughter into his chamber, accompanied by a female judge, for a private counselling session. It was there that he gently encouraged her to meet with me, sensing that despite everything, a thread of our bond still lingered.

Based on what he sensed, he passed a compassionate order that allowed me to meet my daughter for **45 minutes** daily, without any third-party interference.

These daily meetings, over the next two weeks, became a fragile bridge, delicate yet real, offering glimpses of the bond we once shared and the faint hope that it could be restored.

I cannot forget to thank here the Chief Justice and the unknown forces that guided his heart to see beyond legal arguments, into the silent suffering of a mother and daughter separated by manipulation.

On **February 14, 2024,** during the next court hearing, the Chief Justice asked if I wished to stay at the ashram for a few days to understand my daughter's environment better. At that moment, unsure of its implications, I refused the offer and continued to meet her daily under the interim order.

However, after careful thought, driven by the sense of duty and faith that God would guide me, I accepted the proposal during the next hearing on **March 5, 2024.**

Crossing that threshold, I felt faith and fear collide; unaware that the days ahead would demand both in equal measure.

****

CHAPTER IX

Emotional Encounters and Silent Pleas

They promised her freedom, but chained her mind. They promised her heaven, but stole her soul. Yet a mother's love still waits beyond the walls they built.

The ashram where my daughter stayed became both a place of despair and a temporary glimmer of hope for me. Every visit there chipped away at my emotional strength while simultaneously solidifying my determination to bring her back. Despite the unyielding walls, both physical and emotional, that the cult had built around her, I clung to the hope that the light of my heart, which shone for my daughter, could penetrate them.

During our court-mandated 45-minute meetings, from February 1 to February 14, 2024, I tried to reconnect with my daughter. These sessions were my lifeline, but they were also emotionally taxing. Each meeting felt like a battle between her conditioned mind and her true self. Despite the court order prohibiting any third-party interference during my meetings with my daughter, the reality was quite different on the first day. The in-charge and other members of the ashram deliberately walked past the area where we were sitting, their presence a constant reminder that we were being monitored. Their intention was clear: to ensure that my daughter didn't emotionally connect with me.

At one point, the in-charge even approached us and began recording a video, claiming it was necessary to have proof that I had visited the ashram and that they had allowed me inside. This was a calculated move to disrupt the emotional bond I was trying to rebuild with my daughter. The persistent surveillance and interference were deliberate strategies to keep her distracted and emotionally distant.

Frustrated by their blatant disregard for the court's directive, I finally raised my voice and warned them that I would file for contempt of the court's order due to their interference. My threat seemed to have an impact because, from the second day onward, they refrained from any apparent interruptions during my time with my daughter.

For 45 minutes, I brought up memories of our past: the handmade cards she gifted me, the surprises she planned for my birthday every year, and the strength she showed in supporting me through tough times. I reminded her of my struggles as a single parent raising her, how she had been my pillar of strength despite her young age, and how maturely she handled responsibilities when I needed her most. I also spoke of the small, cherished moments, the times we shared food, laughter, love, and gifts, both big and small, the shopping trips where we picked out things together, and how she would demand things from me with the full confidence of being my daughter.

While recounting a painful chapter of my life, emotion overtook me, and I faltered, my voice trembling, unable to contain the flood of pain that surged from within.

For a moment, I saw her facade crack. Her lips quivered, and her eyes glistened with unshed tears.

She looked away, blinking rapidly as if to hold back her emotions.

"Maa, please don't," she said, her voice barely audible. *"This isn't helping either of us."*

In that moment, I saw not the girl they had trained her to be, but my daughter, the one who once held my hand through every storm. Her words may have asked me to stop, but her eyes told another story, a story of love trying to find its way through the fog of confusion. That single flicker of emotion... it was enough to keep my hope alive.

I would often extend my hand toward her, resting it on the dining table between us. My hand silently called out for hers, as it had so many times before. She would look at it, visibly restless.

"Maa, take your hand back," she'd say, her voice tinged with irritation. *"I'm not going to hold it, and it's only hurting you to keep it stretched like that."*

She noticed my hand trembling from the cold and the strain of keeping it extended for so long, as we sat in an open area covered only by grills and curtains. Her concern, though fleeting, revealed a flicker of the daughter I once knew.

Despite these brief glimpses of her true self, the remaining 23 hours and 15 minutes of each day undid my efforts. The cult's teachings reinforced the walls she had built around her emotions, erasing any progress we had made. It felt like building a sandcastle only to see it washed away by relentless waves.

During those days, the police told me my daughter had claimed she'd returned the phone and laptop she'd taken from home. I paused; not because of the lie itself, but because of how effortlessly she spoke it. This was never about devices; it was about watching Laaddo, my child, raised on honesty, love, and trust, stand before me, echoing someone else's words. She wasn't speaking from her heart but reciting a carefully constructed script that left no room for our shared past.

I confronted her, calm at first. *"You told the police you returned my laptop and phone."* She nodded, avoiding my eyes. Her lips tightened; her posture stiffened. In a barely audible voice, she repeated, *"I did."* There was no warmth, no mother–daughter bond, only a rehearsed statement. I saw guilt flicker behind her eyes before it was buried under her training to obey. In that moment, I realized this lie wasn't about a device, but about how far they had pulled her away from herself; a takeover of her thoughts, her truth, her very choices.

On February 13, assuming it might be my last meeting with her before the court's next hearing, I spoke to her with a heavy heart.

"Laaddo, congratulations," I said, my voice trembling. *"You've reserved a place in Satyug, leaving behind your useless mother."*

Her eyes softened, and she replied with a quiet conviction that broke me. *"Aap bhi Satyug mein chaloge mere saath, kyunki aap meri maa ho."* (You will also go to Satyug with me, because you are my mother.)

Her words, though steeped in the cult's teachings, revealed her undying love for me. At that moment, I felt both despair and hope, despair at how deeply she was conditioned, and hope that her love for me still lingered beneath it all.

*****

My stay at the ashram:

As per the court's order of **March 5**, the very next morning, I had to travel from my place of residence to the place she was staying. I was not someone who could easily manage going anywhere alone, especially in a vast, unfamiliar city like Delhi. Even in normal situations, I often found myself confused in small lanes. And now, with my mind clouded, my heart heavy, and my consciousness barely cooperating with me, I was totally blank. At the bus stop, I noticed a man waiting for the bus. Striking up a conversation, he told me he was heading to the same destination. Not only did he guide me after we got off the bus, but he also led me exactly through the right lane, as if he had been sent to assist me in that very moment of helplessness.

In a city as vast as Delhi, filled with countless bus stops and confusing lanes, such a coincidence felt nothing short of divine intervention. It was as if God had sent an angel to help me at a moment when I needed it.

While walking forward, I was lost and confused about what the outcome would be. The thought of spending a week in that oppressive environment, where the cult had its grip on every corner, filled me with unease. However, the opportunity to understand the depth of her control pushed me to go ahead with the plan.

Standing outside that cage-like triple-storeyed building, I reminded myself,

"This is not the time to doubt, this is the time to act, to believe, and to prepare myself for a positive outcome."

The first day at the ashram was overwhelming. As soon as I stepped inside, I was told that I wasn't allowed to use my mobile on the second floor where they all used to reside. I was struck by the cold, sterile atmosphere, a stark contrast to the warmth I had always known. Yet, a part of me clung to hope, hoping that somehow, I could reach her, even if just for a brief instant.

As I spent more time with my child, the emotional distance became more apparent. The walls she had built under the cult's influence were impenetrable. The warmth I had always offered her was rejected, and every attempt to connect felt like an act of futility. But beneath that, I could feel the echo of my Laaddo I once knew, the girl who had laughed, who had shared her dreams with me, a part of whom was waiting to return home. My heart ached with longing to break through, to remind her of who she truly was before this foreign influence took hold.

Throughout those seven days, I observed the meticulous control exerted over my Laaddo and the other girls in the ashram. Every aspect of their lives had been regimented, down to the smallest detail. The routine was designed to keep the followers in a constant state of activity and submission, with little opportunity for personal thought or reflection.

I noticed that all communication within the premises was tightly controlled. Conversations were brief and formal, as if emotions were something to be avoided. The followers spoke to each other with a sense of detachment, like robotic responses rather than genuine human interactions. They were often instructed not to engage in unnecessary discussions, especially about their personal lives. Even the most basic social interactions seemed devoid of warmth or comfort.

The entire atmosphere felt sterile, devoid of any color or personal touches. The walls bore posters of their teachings and motivational quotes encouraging dedication to the cult's ideology. The furniture was sparse, and the energy in the rooms was cold and oppressive. There were no decorations, no personal items, and certainly no signs of individuality. Everything seemed designed to strip away any remnants of personal identity and replace them with uniformity and obedience to the cult's teachings.

Amol, who was always in the background, ensured that all of this took place under his watchful eyes. His influence was invisible but pervasive, like an unspoken rule that governed every movement and action.

One evening, I overheard a conversation between two followers. They spoke in hushed tones, but I could still make out their words. They were discussing how they had been chosen for a *"higher purpose"* and how questioning the cult's teachings would lead to ruin. It was as though they believed the world outside the ashram no longer mattered, as if they had already transcended everything else. I shuddered at the thought that this was how my daughter had been conditioned to see the world.

My daughter and I were permitted to stay together in a small, dimly lit room on the ground floor. The atmosphere was stifling, and every movement we made seemed to be under surveillance. At night, I'd try to talk to her, but the emotional walls she had built were impenetrable.

She insisted on keeping the lights on throughout the night, explaining that darkness allowed negative energies to thrive.
"The souls around us might attack," she said with conviction. The fear they had instilled in her was palpable, and she was completely consumed by it.

On the early morning of the second day, as I sat beside her during their morning rituals of meditation and preachings of VDD, they listened to, the chill in the air seeped into my bones. My feet were numb, aching with cold. She sat next to me, wrapped tightly in a warm blanket, her posture composed yet distant, eyes closed in a trance-like state.

Instinctively, like I had done so many times during her childhood winters, I reached out to her warmth; not to disturb, not to intrude, just to share a sliver of comfort. I gently slid my icy feet under the edge of her blanket.

In an instant, she recoiled.

"Don't, Maa. You're not supposed to touch me," she hissed, her voice sharp and urgent, laced with fear more than anger.

The words, simple yet foreign, sliced through the silence. My heart clenched. I froze, not from the cold this time, but from the sting of her rejection. It wasn't just the blanket she had pulled away; it was herself.

Her tone wasn't hers; it was rehearsed, mechanical. And yet, it hit me like a slap. A slap that didn't bruise the skin but bruised something far deeper; a sacred bond being overwritten.
That one sentence carried a thousand unspoken ones: *"You don't belong*

here," "You're not one of us," "You're untouchable now."

I sat there, stunned, trying to focus on the things around me, but my ears buzzed with her voice.

My daughter, my child, was now drawing boundaries I didn't understand. Not physical, but emotional, spiritual, invisible lines drawn by someone else's beliefs. And I, her mother, was now a stranger crossing them.

At one point, my daughter told me that her real mother is Kamla Devi, the woman whom VDD had once given the title of "Jagadamba". She said that Kamla Devi has forgotten her divine role for now but will soon return to accept her as her true child. The heartbreaking irony is that Kamla Devi is living her life peacefully with her own family, completely unaware of my daughter's existence.

(**Note:** Kamla Devi Dixit was the first girl surrendered to VDD in 1983 at around 13 years of age. Declared "Jagdamba", mother of mankind. She was called his creation, while he claimed to be the creator. After VDD's arrest in 1998, she distanced herself from the cult, got married in 2000, and now lives happily with her husband and two children. Despite her clear dissociation, cult followers continue to misuse her name, falsely claiming that she will return by 2028, a claim she has publicly denied in a YouTube video. "*Kamaladevi message only for PBKs*")

Meanwhile, I, her real mother in this life, who gave birth to her, raised her, and loves her more than life itself, was suddenly disqualified from that role. She was told, and made to reaffirm that I'm her mother only for this birth, while she awaits the return of a woman who doesn't even know her.

As if that weren't painful enough, she also revealed that Kamla Devi plans to first provoke the followers against VDD as a test to see who remains dedicated. According to her belief, only those who pass this test will be safe and survive when destruction comes.

And here I am... a mother longing for her child, cast aside, while she chases an illusion created by the very people who stole her away from me.

The paranoia extended to every corner of her life. Windows were covered with heavy curtains, and the terrace was shielded to ensure no one could look out or be seen. Followers weren't allowed to leave the premises unaccompanied. Even walking from one floor to another required permission and a companion.

Moreover, the repeated teachings that even one's own father or brother could turn into a *Duryodhana* or *Dushasana* in Kalyug had deeply embedded themselves in her mind; messages I had often heard echoed by my cousins.

That conditioning had taken a visible form in her behavior.

My daughter was never allowed to go to the ground floor or the terrace alone; she always had to be accompanied, as though trusting anyone, even in the most routine situations, could lead to her downfall. If, by chance, she crossed paths with a man, such as the husband of the ashram in-charge who lived on the first floor, while moving from the second floor to the ground floor, she would instantly turn her face away. The accompanying mataji would immediately inform him of her presence, prompting him to retreat to avoid any direct encounter. It resembled the old orthodox custom, where a newlywed daughter-in-law turns her face and avoids eye contact upon seeing her father-in-law. In this situation, it wasn't tradition but fear and indoctrination that dictated her actions.

Her daily routine was grueling. She woke up at 2:40 AM for meditation, a practice they referred to as *"Amritwela Yog."* The rest of her day was filled with chores, sermons, and other activities designed to keep her mind occupied and prevent her from questioning the reality around her. Even meals were eaten in silence, with followers encouraged to focus only on their inner thoughts.

I noticed how utterly exhausted she was. The lack of proper sleep and the constant mental pressure were taking a visible toll on her. Yet, she seemed oblivious to her deteriorating health.

"This is my purusharth, Maa. You wouldn't understand," she said when I expressed concern.

As if this suffocating control over her movements wasn't enough, they went a step further. They poisoned my daughter's mind against me. They filled her heart with suspicion and fear, making her believe that her own mother was practicing black magic to bring her back. They claimed I had spilled something sinister on the ashram premises, something meant to harm or manipulate her spiritually. And as a supposed shield against these "dark energies," they tied a black thread around her wrist, convincing her that it would protect her from my so-called spells. That simple thread, which should have been a symbol of faith or tradition, became a barrier between a mother and her child, feeding the illusion that I was her enemy, not her protector.

On the sixth day, I found a fleeting opportunity to interact with the daughter of the lady in charge, a young girl of just 17 years. I saw a fragile thread of innocence still alive in her. Hoping to hold up a mirror for my daughter, I gently initiated a conversation.

I asked her gently, *"How old are you?"*

When she told me, I smiled and said softly, *"Once you turn 18, you'll be free to see the world for yourself. It's not as harsh as it's made out to be. There's so much beauty outside, nature, life, people."*

Then, after a pause, I added, *"If you ever need help... I'll be there, for support, for strength, just to help you stand on your own."*

Before I could finish, my daughter's voice cut through the air, sharp and angry. She accused me of provoking the young girl.

What she could not see was that I was only holding up a reflection for her; the same reflection she once unknowingly stood before. They had planted the same seed in her innocent heart: that the moment she turned 18, she would have the absolute freedom to choose, and that their world was true salvation.

I wanted her to recognize how easy it was to manipulate a pure soul under the guise of *"freedom."* I wanted her to understand that she was never to blame; it was their careful, calculated exploitation of her natural desire for independence that had led her astray.

But at that moment, she could not see it. Her mind, shaped and shielded by their conditioning, remained captive. The cult's psychological grip ran so deep that she no longer believed her own mother could be trusted. The seeds of doubt they had planted had grown into rigid walls of suspicion and fear.

On the seventh day, I gathered all my strength and spoke to her patiently. I told her openly that I had deliberately initiated that conversation with the young girl, not to provoke, but to gently reflect a truth she had once lived through. I explained that I was trying to hold up a mirror, hoping she might recognize the same vulnerability in that girl that once existed in her.

Then, cautiously, I played her an audio recording of Amol. I pointed out the manipulative undertones in his words, trying to help her understand the intent behind his seemingly spiritual guidance. For a moment, I saw a flicker of surprise in her eyes. She listened hesitantly, but she listened. I also showed her some disturbing clips of VDD. She seemed unsettled, perhaps even confused. Her gaze shifted; her thoughts stirred. For a few moments, I felt she was trying to piece things together, trying to make sense of the cracks in the illusion.

But the moment was fleeting.

Within minutes, it was as though a switch had flipped. Her expression hardened again. She straightened her posture, her voice regained firmness, and with deep conviction, she said, *"I am on the right path, Maa. One day, you will see it too."*

That brief glimmer of openness was gone, snatched back by the powerful hold of the narratives they had etched into her mind. The conditioning was still stronger than any truth I could offer.

As her words settled in the air, I felt a quiet ache rise within me. That fleeting moment of vulnerability, where I thought I had reached her, vanished like a mirage. It was like watching the door to her heart crack open just a little, only to be slammed shut again. The pain wasn't in her resistance; it was in knowing that she was still trapped, unable to see the difference between love and control.

After all these efforts, finally, the day had arrived to move out, without any result. I had come every day with hope in my eyes and prayers in my heart, but I was leaving with nothing but silence and unanswered questions. Still, somewhere deep within, a mother's faith refused to fade. I left the place physically, but a part of me stayed behind with her.

****

CHAPTER X

The Fight for Truth: Building a Case

When truth becomes a battlefield, persistence becomes prayer, and love becomes the sharpest weapon against deception.

The path ahead was uncharted, fraught with uncertainty and the weight of emotional turmoil. The Chief Justice's recognition of my daughter's conditioned behavior gave me a glimmer of hope, but the road to reclaiming her was going to be long and arduous.

Every court hearing felt like an eternity. While the evidence of manipulation and coercion was piling up, the judicial system's pace was painfully slow. Each adjournment, each delayed decision, felt like another day lost to the cult's influence over my daughter. The realization that the system, bound by its processes, couldn't provide immediate relief was frustrating and disheartening.

"A mother spends years teaching her child to walk, speak, and think, but the law won't even allow her to ask if the child is walking into darkness."

I had presented ample evidence: WhatsApp chats, emails, and testimonies, showing how my daughter was manipulated. Yet, the defense's counterarguments and delays stretched the proceedings. I couldn't help but feel that justice was slipping through my fingers.

In moments of despair, I reminded myself of why I was fighting. My daughter wasn't just a victim of manipulation; she was my world. The bond we shared, the sacrifices we made for each other, and the love that once defined our relationship fueled my determination.

Each time I entered the courtroom, I carried with me the memories of her childhood, her laughter, curiosity, and unwavering love for me. These memories were my strength, my reminder that the person I was fighting for still existed beneath the layers of indoctrination.

Understanding the cult's operations became my top priority. To deepen my understanding, I read the book *"Combating Cult Mind Control"* by Steven Hassan, who was a mental health counselor and cult expert offering insights into how destructive cults manipulate individuals, whose insights offered me a lot of clarity.

I began reaching out to ex-members who had managed to escape, carefully documenting their experiences and the psychological patterns of coercion they had endured. Each testimony painted a disturbing picture of how the cult preyed on emotional vulnerability, gradually manipulating individuals into severing ties with their families and surrendering their autonomy.

To my utter surprise, all the points of manipulation explained in the book were exactly followed by VDD and then by Amol, which typically include:

1. **Isolation from Family and Friends:** Members are encouraged to cut ties with loved ones, creating emotional dependency on the cult.
2. **Identity Reformation:** The follower's personal identity is replaced with a cult-assigned role through new names, clothing, rituals, or groupthink.
3. **Induced Dependency and Obedience:** Members are made to believe they cannot survive or achieve salvation without the cult or its leader, fostering blind obedience.
4. **Thought-Stopping Techniques:** Doubts and critical thinking are suppressed through chanting, mantras, or rigid belief systems that discourage questioning.
5. **Fear and Guilt Manipulation:** Followers are controlled through the fear of punishment, guilt over their past or present, and a constant sense of unworthiness.
6. **Controlled Information Flow:** Access to outside information is restricted, isolating members from alternative perspectives and reinforcing the cult's narrative.
7. **Charismatic or Narcissistic Leader:** The leader demands absolute loyalty and is seen as divine, enlightened, or the sole bearer of truth.
8. **Apocalyptic Fear and Exclusive Salvation:** Cults often promote the belief that the world will soon be destroyed and only their members will survive or be saved, intensifying fear and reinforcing exclusivity.

Cults use this systematic set of psychological tactics to manipulate and control their followers.

Upon reviewing the AIVV website (pbks.info), I found it deeply disturbing; its FAQs were misleading and evasive, merely beating around the bush instead of addressing substantive concerns.

The Hidden Empire:

How VDD Built a Cult Around a Divine Delusion:

Virendra Dev Dixit (VDD), formerly associated with the *Brahma Kumaris*, was beaten and expelled from the organization after he began claiming that he was *"Lord Shiva"* incarnated in a human body. He challenged the core belief of the Brahma Kumaris by asserting that Dada Lekhraj was not the complete medium of Shiva. Instead, he declared himself to be the true incarnation, the permanent chariot of Lord Shiva. Following his expulsion, he went on to establish his own group, the **Adhyatmik Vishwa Vidyalaya (AIVV),** promoting his distinct interpretation of spiritual teachings. His teachings altered and extended the Brahma Kumaris' doctrine, under the guise of advanced spiritual knowledge.

He asserted that his mission was to enlighten the world. He proclaimed that he would never die, that he would lead his followers into Satyuga through his very own body. He spoke of an impending *pralay*, a great destruction where the rest of the world would perish, while his devotees would remain untouched, shielded by divine power. According to his narrative, they would be buried in ice during this cataclysm, only to awaken when the ice melted with the arrival of Satyuga. At that moment, he claimed, his followers would return to life, transformed and radiant, possessing what he called *"kanchan kaya",* a golden, immortal body, and elevate them to the divine status of Raja and Rani. These grand promises painted a picture of divine privilege, drawing vulnerable hearts into a fantasy of salvation, while subtly severing their ties with reality.

His system demanded absolute submission; followers were expected to relinquish their mental autonomy, emotional independence, physical bodies, wealth, and time in the name of spiritual progress. His doctrine was meticulously designed to foster dependency, enforce constant self-surveillance, and maintain tight control through fear and guilt.

One of the most disturbing aspects of VDD's teachings was how he specifically targeted young women to reinforce his power:

- **Demonizing Maternal Bonds:** VDD taught that a young woman's greatest spiritual obstacle was her attachment to her mother. By portraying the maternal bond as a barrier to enlightenment, he systematically weakened one of the most natural and protective relationships in a woman's life, pushing her into emotional isolation and deeper dependence on him.
- **Demanding Total Physical Surrender:** Beyond emotional control, VDD emphasized that true spiritual advancement required female followers to offer complete physical surrender. This blurring of spiritual instruction with physical exploitation exposed the darker, predatory motives behind his so-called teachings.
- **Creating an "All-or-Nothing" Paradigm:** His framework left no space for balance or questioning. Any hesitation was labeled as weakness or sin, forcing followers to believe that only total compliance would lead to salvation, while any deviation meant spiritual death.

Over time, multiple allegations of sexual exploitation, illegal confinement, and abuse began to surface against VDD. Investigations revealed shocking testimonies from survivors who had managed to escape his clutches. As pressure mounted and law enforcement agencies closed in, VDD absconded in 2017–2018, evading arrest and disappearing from public view. Since then, he has been a fugitive, with multiple cases pending against him and the Central Bureau of Investigation (CBI) continuing to pursue him.,

After his disappearance, leadership struggles and power tussles erupted within the organization. Without VDD's direct control, his followers split into factions, each vying for authority, finances, and the "legacy" of the cult.

One figure to emerge from this chaos was **Amol**, who had earlier served as VDD's legal advocate. Seizing the opportunity, Amol formed a separate group, presenting himself as a faithful propagator of VDD's teachings. He claimed to be carrying forward VDD's "sewa" and has been systematically attempting to replicate all of VDD's practices. Amol further indoctrinates followers with the belief that VDD's children, meaning the devotees raised under his ideology, will eventually assume leadership roles and perpetuate his mission in his absence.

Thus, even though VDD physically absconded, the machinery of manipulation he had constructed continued to evolve, mutate, and entrap new lives under the guise of spiritual salvation.

A Tool of Entrapment: The Surrender Affidavit

AIVV's control wasn't built on faith alone; it was fortified through legally binding documents that stripped individuals of their autonomy and tethered them indefinitely. Chief among these tools of entrapment was the Surrender Affidavit, a chilling document that turned a personal decision into a life sentence.

This affidavit wasn't merely a declaration of faith; it was a weapon that isolated individuals from their families, robbed them of their legal standing, and left them vulnerable to manipulation and exploitation. The format of which is as follows:

<u>AFFIDAVIT OF SURRENDER OF VIRGIN</u>

Date: xxxxxxx

In the presence of: Shivbaba c/o Prajapita Brahma
Through the Affidavit: I, xxxxxxxxxxx, D/O: xxxxxxxx
Date of Birth-xx-xx-xxxx, Age-xx,
R/o- xxxxxxxxxxxxxxxxxxx Colony, Hyderabad 500 044, solemnly affirm & declare as following:

1. I bear the abovementioned name and address and I am well aware of the contents of this Affidavit.
2. After listening, thinking-churning and the deep study of Shivbaba's Murlis narrated through Dada Lekhraj Brahma and the Avyakt Vanis narrated by the divine soul of Dada Lekhraj (Brahma) through the medium of Gulzar Dadi, published by the Brahmakumari Ishwariya Vishwavidyalaya, Mount Abu, and as per my personal experience, I have firm faith, confidence and strong faith that the practical initial part of the household path of the Supreme Father Supreme Soul Point of Light Shiva, has been revealed in the form of Jagadamba-Jagatpita (Durga-Shankar) through Kamla Devi Dikshit and Virendra Dev Dikshit respectively at Adhyatmik Vishwavidyalaya, village & post- Kampila, District-Farrukhabad (Uttar Pradesh).
3. I consider these two as my spiritual parents, I solemnly pledge to remain celibate throughout my life and to follow Shivbaba's Shrimat.
4. My date of birth according to my High School certificate is xx-xx-xxxx and age is xx years.

5. I am a major girl, and I am entitled to right to Religious freedom, right to stay and reside anywhere in India as per the Indian Constitution and I can spend my life in Godly service at Adhyatmik Vishwavidyalaya.

6. Accordingly, I voluntarily surrender myself by the body, mind and wealth in this Divine Yagya of the knowledge of Shivbaba for my entire lifetime, without any undue pressure, by staking all my relationships happily with pure Indian religious feelings, with the purpose of studying the spiritual knowledge and Divine services.

7. I will always follow the special Divine Shrimat received through Brahma regarding eating and drinking, living, conduct and behaviour and I shall never use physical power on anyone against Shrimat.

8. I have not been married to anyone. I am a virgin. If any marital relationship is proved in future, then my **Surrender letter** be considered as invalid.

9. I am not suffering from any chronic and severe disease (like T.B, Cancer, HIV, Hepatitis B, Leprosy, etc.) If I am found suffering from any of such severe diseases in the future, then my **Surrender letter** be considered as invalid.

10. There are no debts incurred on me. If any debt is found in future, then my **Surrender letter** be considered as invalid.

11. No case is pending in any Court against me and there isn't any complaint in the Police Station either.

Signature and thumb impression of the Deponent

Verification: According to my personal knowledge and belief I pledge that the facts described in the paragraph 1 to 11 in this affidavit to be correct and true. No facts have been concealed and nothing is false either.

Signature and thumb impression of the Deponent

WITNESSES:

1. xxxxx
2. xxxxx

*****

Key Clauses of the Surrender Affidavit:

1. **Declaration of Virginity and Fitness:** Recruits were compelled to declare their virginity, marital status, and lack of chronic illnesses such as HIV, tuberculosis, or cancer. These intrusive requirements not only invaded their personal lives but also gave VDD the leverage to exploit

their vulnerabilities, using these declarations to control them emotionally and physically.

2. **Complete Devotion – "Tann, Mann, and Dhann":** The affidavit demanded the offering of one's body (Tann), mind (Mann), and wealth (Dhann) to VDD. Members were pressured to surrender their material possessions, including jewelry, property, and savings, under the guise of spiritual service. This left them financially dependent and trapped, with no means to rebuild their lives if they ever tried to leave.

3. **Waiver of Accountability:** By signing the affidavit, members absolved VDD of any responsibility for harm caused to them. This provision cleverly shifted all liability to the victims, effectively silencing dissent and discouraging any legal action, as they had willingly agreed to the terms.

The clauses in the affidavit were more than just words on paper, they were chains binding individuals to the cult's control. Members, particularly young women, were coerced into signing these documents without fully comprehending the long-term implications. Once signed, the affidavit became a psychological and legal tool to suppress any attempt at resistance or escape.

Stories of others trapped:

(Note: To protect the privacy and dignity of those involved, a few names of individuals, especially the young victims, have been changed, except in the case of Amol, who continues to hold a position of influence within the organization and whose actions are already a matter of public concern, along with his channel "Spiritual revolution". This book seeks not to target individuals, but to bring awareness, share truth, and protect others from similar pain.)

One victim, Seema, shared her harrowing experience with the surrender affidavit:

> *"Once you step inside the ashram, you are required to hand over all your electronic devices. Communication with your family or friends is completely cut off, even if you wish to reach out. They remind you of the oath taken through the surrender affidavit, making it a nightmare for anyone trapped inside. Changing your mind is not an option. If you express a desire to leave, they intimidate you by*

invoking the affidavit. The atmosphere inside is suffocating, with closed windows and curtains that block out the world. There's no freedom, no ventilation, and an overwhelming sense of confinement.

The mediators exploit young minds by convincing them that this affidavit is a sacred contract between themselves and God. They promise divine rewards for their sacrifice, but the reality is far from it. Girls are used for spreading the VDD's teachings, but only as long as they are physically fit. Once deemed unfit due to illness or age, they are discarded without any compensation or care. Many are left to fend for themselves, homeless and penniless, with no career or family to fall back on."

The stories of those who signed the surrender affidavit underscore the urgent need for change. The affidavit exploited the naivety of young minds, emphasizing chronological age over emotional and intellectual maturity. As one victim put it:

"IQ and maturity of thought should be considered, not just the age of 18, to determine if someone is truly capable of making life-altering decisions."

The affidavit turned a deep personal choice into a binding, one-sided agreement that left its victims powerless. It is a stark reminder of how legal tools, when misused, can become instruments of exploitation rather than protection.

*****

The Scientist Who Gave Up Everything

One of VDD's most heartbreaking victims was Dr. Rekha, a brilliant scientist who had once worked in the USA. Lured by promises of spiritual awakening and a higher purpose, she gave up her prestigious career and returned to India in 2015, only to surrender herself completely to the cult. Her transformation was swift and complete.

Her elderly parents, devastated and confused, left their hometown and moved to Delhi in the hope of rescuing their daughter. Unfamiliar with language, they struggled in an unfamiliar city, living in a cramped room on the second floor for nearly a decade. Both of them faced serious health issues, but their only concern was their daughter's return. They exhausted their life savings in a long and painful legal battle, hoping to bring her back.

Despite their sacrifices and years of unwavering effort, Rekha remained deeply entrenched in the cult's ideology. Her indifference toward her aging parents, who gave everything to see her safe, stands as a painful reminder of how manipulation can not only cloud judgment but also numb emotional ties. Her story is a tragic example of how even the most educated and accomplished individuals can fall victim when their inner vulnerabilities are exploited.

*****

The Girl Who Lost Her Voice:

At just 14 years old, in 2004, Lakshmi was forced by her parents to surrender herself to AIVV, believing it was a path to spiritual growth. What she didn't realize was that this decision would lead her into a living nightmare. Under the manipulation of Virendra Dev Dixit (VDD), she was coerced into surrendering her body with the false promise of spiritual liberation. Instead, she endured years of trauma, her voice silenced, her identity erased. Her life became a quiet prison, governed by the cult's distorted beliefs.

The horror didn't end there. Lakshmi was threatened that if she ever spoke out against the abuse, she would be punished in her next life by becoming deaf and dumb. The psychological manipulation left her unable to rebuild her life or even speak out for fear of the consequences.

*****

The Final Goodbye That Never Came:

In 1996, a young woman named Pooja surrendered herself to AIVV at the age of just 20, believing she was choosing a higher spiritual path. Over the next 23 years, she was moved from one ashram to another, deliberately cut off from the outside world. Her family tried desperately to meet her, but every attempt was blocked. Letters, visits, and even pleas were all turned away by the cult's rigid control.

In 2013, tragedy struck when her mother passed away. Five years later, her father also died. Heartbreakingly, Pooja was never informed about either loss. She remained trapped in the belief system AIVV had built around her, unaware of the tragedies unfolding outside.

It wasn't until 2019, after a long internal struggle, that she managed to leave AIVV. Only then did she learn the devastating truth: her parents were gone, and she had been denied the chance to say goodbye.

The years she lost, the bonds that were broken, and the grief of being absent at the most crucial moments left deep emotional scars. Though she reclaimed her freedom, the pain of lost time and missed final moments with her parents would forever remain with her.

*****

Fighting AIVV for Father and Home:

Eluri Shyam Sunder, from Tadepalligudem, Andhra Pradesh, tells the tragic story of his family's victimization by VDD and his cult, AIVV. In the late 1990s, Shyam Sunder's father, seeking to overcome bad habits, joined Brahmakumaris and later became involved with VDD's cult. Over the years, the cult manipulated and isolated Shyam Sunder's father, convincing him to lease the family's property to them for extended periods without the family's consent.

VDD's followers took advantage of these fraudulent leases and hid Shyam Sunder's father, preventing his family from contacting him. Despite their legal battles, including attempts to regain their property and bring their father home, the cult's influence continued. Shyam Sunder's mother passed away in 2013, and his older brother in 2022, while their father remained under VDD's control.

Shyam Sunder is now fighting in the courts to annul the fraudulent lease agreements and expose VDD's fraudulent activities. His petition calls for the immediate arrest of VDD and the closure of his organization, demanding justice and the reunion of families torn apart by the cult's manipulation.

*****

Vanita's Story: A Battle for Her Sister's Freedom:

In 2015, Vanita and her younger sister joined AIVV together, drawn by its promises of salvation and a new world. While Vanita eventually recognized the deception and managed to escape in 2018, her sister remained deeply trapped under the organization's influence.

In 2023, tragedy struck when their father passed away. Vanita, heartbroken but determined, fought tirelessly to bring her sister back home for the funeral. The AIVV followers tried to manipulate her sister, telling her that the death of a parent was insignificant, calling him merely a "connection in this lifetime", not worth mourning.

Despite their efforts to emotionally detach her, Vanita's persistence and unconditional love finally prevailed. She succeeded in bringing her sister back, giving their father the respect and farewell he deserved.

However, the emotional trauma and psychological battle left deep scars on Vanita and her family. Her story reflects the heartbreaking reality of how deeply AIVV's manipulation can sever even the strongest family bonds, and the immense courage it takes to reclaim them.

*****

Why Many Victims Stay Silent:

For every story that surfaced, countless others remained untold. Many victims, especially those coerced into surrendering their bodies, live with the shame and trauma of their experiences. They fear societal judgment and often lack the evidence or resources to pursue justice.

Others, drained by years of manipulation and legal battles, choose to remain silent, hoping to find peace in the years they are left with. The cult's methods of control, psychological manipulation, financial dependence, and legal entrapment create a fortress of silence around its victims.

A Cry for Justice:

Listening to these stories deepened my purpose. My daughter's plight was not an isolated case, it was part of a broader, deeply entrenched system of exploitation. Each story added fuel to my fight, reminding me that this battle wasn't just for her but for every victim silenced by fear, shame, or despair.

Their pain became my strength, their silence my call to action. If I could fight for my daughter, perhaps I could pave the way for others to reclaim their lives as well.

****

CHAPTER XI

From Shadows to Solidarity

From silence rose a whisper; from a whisper, a movement.

As my daughter was drawn deeper into the fold, she was made to believe she wasn't just a follower, she was a chosen one. A messenger of a divine mission. They filled her heart with purpose, urging her to share this so-called 'ultimate truth' with others, especially her friends from school and college. She spoke with unshakable conviction, her eyes shining with a borrowed light, unaware that she was being used in a larger, darker design.

Some of her friends, bright, trusting teenagers, began to show interest. A few even started interacting with Amol's followers, without their parents ever knowing. These weren't strangers. They were children I had once taught. Students I had watched giggle in school corridors, now slipping silently into an unseen web.

When my daughter left home, the grief was deep, but a mother's love holds steady even in the darkest moments. I began reaching out to the other children, not to challenge them, but to understand what they had been led to believe. I listened with patience and shared what I had come to know, not to shake their faith, but to offer another perspective, one rooted in care and truth.

One of the first ideas they were taught was that they are souls, not daughters, not sons, and that all relationships in this birth are temporary. This belief was used to slowly detach them from their families, as if love and bonds were distractions from a higher calling.

And I told them, gently but honestly:

"*True guidance brings clarity, not confusion. It respects your freedom, not demands your silence.*"

Some listened. Some stepped away. A few quietly chose a different path. I may never know the full impact of those conversations, but I know it was important to speak. And I will keep going for as long as there's even one soul caught in silence, still waiting to be heard.

*****

One day, as usual, Amol conducted a spiritual session at a well-known school and proudly posted it on his YouTube channel, 'Spiritual revolution.' I could no longer stay silent. I visited the school. I met the principal. I showed them the truth behind the polished language and serene visuals. The principal was stunned and deeply grateful. They thanked me for bringing it to their attention.

But that was just one school. Amol didn't stop. His sessions are still continuing, in new towns, cities all over the country. Almost every other day, he enters schools, speaking to students, planting the same seeds, quietly, strategically, persistently.

That's when I realized this cannot remain a solitary battle. I am just one mother. But this is no longer only about my daughter. This is about every child. Every parent. Every teacher. Every school. Every guardian of young minds who believes that innocence must be protected.

I need support. We need a movement. Educators, Legal experts, Psychologists, Digital safety experts, and Aware citizens.

We must come together, not only to stop one man's manipulation, but to safeguard the minds of those who have not yet been taken in, but are dangerously close.

This is a call for awareness.

A call for action.

A call for collective courage.

If you're reading this and your heart stirs, then this message is for you.

Let this book not end with my voice alone.

Let it rise with yours.

Let it become a movement born not out of anger, but out of love.

Out of solidarity. From shadows, into light.

An Open Letter: A Message to all the stakeholders:

To Parents:

Dear parents, my story is not just a tale of personal loss and struggle; it's a cautionary tale for all of us. Our children are our most precious treasures, but they are also vulnerable, especially during their formative years when they are searching for meaning, identity, and purpose. This search often leads them into unknown territories, and sometimes, into the hands of those who exploit their innocence and trust.

Please pay attention to the subtle changes in your children. Are they becoming unusually withdrawn? Are they engaging in conversations that seem rehearsed or influenced? Are they spending excessive time on their phones or laptops, building connections with people they don't know? These could be signs of external manipulation.

But beyond observation, the key is building a foundation of trust and communication within your family. Create an environment where your children feel safe sharing their thoughts, dreams, and even their fears with you. Listen to them without judgment. Make them feel heard and valued so that they are less likely to seek validation or belong elsewhere.

Understand that manipulation doesn't always come in the form of obvious threats or coercion. Sometimes, it is disguised as spirituality, self-improvement, or a promise of a better life. It's easy to dismiss early signs as mere phases or harmless interests, but being vigilant and involved in their lives can make all the difference. Be their anchor in a world full of distractions and uncertainties.

To Society:

As a society, we cannot afford to remain silent or indifferent. Organizations that exploit individuals under the guise of spirituality, enlightenment, or salvation thrive in the shadows. They prey on the vulnerable, those seeking answers, healing, or a sense of belonging. And they flourish because we, as a community, often choose to look the other way.

It's time to break the silence. Awareness is our strongest weapon against these exploitative cults. Let's talk about them. Let's share stories of those who have been affected. Let's together support families who are fighting to rescue their loved ones. Let's demand stricter regulations and accountability against organizations operating under the guise of spirituality.

But beyond just combating cults, we need to foster a culture where emotional and mental well-being are prioritized. Teach our youth critical thinking skills so that they can recognize manipulation. Encourage open dialogue about spirituality, faith, and personal growth, so they are not drawn to extremist ideologies in search of answers.

We have a moral responsibility to protect the vulnerable, especially our youth, from falling prey to such dark forces. Together, through collective awareness, education, and action, we can dismantle the hold these cults have on individuals and families.

To Schools, Colleges, and Authorities:

To ensure the safety and well-being of students, it is crucial to **screen all visiting speakers** thoroughly. This involves verifying their background, understanding the true purpose of their visit, and identifying any affiliations they may have with external organizations. No individual should be allowed to conduct talks or workshops without proper vetting and approval by the school administration.

Schools must also enforce a strict policy to **prevent unsupervised access to students,** particularly when it is done under the pretext of spirituality, personality development, or similar activities. All interactions with students by external visitors should be closely monitored by responsible faculty members.

There is a growing need to **introduce workshops on cult awareness** as part of teacher training and student well-being programs. These workshops can help educators, counselors, and students recognize early signs of psychological manipulation, undue influence, and coercive persuasion tactics often used by harmful groups.

Additionally, the institution should **create anonymous reporting channels** that allow students, teachers, or parents to raise concerns without fear of retaliation. This will empower the school community to speak up if they notice any suspicious behavior or influence.

Lastly, schools must **insist on parental involvement** in any extracurricular guidance related to spirituality, counseling, or mentorship. No external spiritual mentorship or life coaching should be allowed without the informed consent and understanding of the student's family, ensuring that parents remain fully aware of their child's influences and environment.

To the Government of India:

Respected Authorities,
I write this not as a victim, but as a mother who is fighting for justice, not just for her daughter, but for many others who remain unheard. The

growing influence of manipulative cults in India is no longer a hidden issue. It is silently swallowing the emotional, psychological, and even physical freedom of our youth.

India has no cult-specific laws, and though crimes can be prosecuted, **victims often struggle to get justice** due to delays, disbelief, or political pressure.

Countries like France, Japan, and Germany have acknowledged this threat and acted with legal and structural safeguards. I ask, **why is India still silent?**

Global Legal Approaches to Curbing Cult Influence

The threat posed by manipulative cults is not confined to one country; it is a global concern. Nations across the world have responded in various ways, implementing laws and policies to protect their citizens from psychological exploitation, financial fraud, and the erosion of fundamental rights. These legal frameworks, however, differ significantly in intent and execution, reflecting the unique cultural, political, and constitutional values of each society.

France: Balancing Freedom and Protection:

France has long taken a proactive stance against cultic deviations. In 2001, it enacted the *About–Picard Law*, a landmark piece of legislation designed to dismantle organizations that undermine human dignity and freedoms. This law empowers courts to dissolve groups found guilty of serious crimes like mental manipulation, fraud, or endangerment of life. Though widely supported by victim advocacy groups, the law has also faced criticism from religious freedom advocates, who argue that it may be used to target minority faiths unfairly. Despite this, France remains firm in its commitment to protect vulnerable individuals from exploitative systems, with the government-backed MIVILUDES agency serving as a central force in monitoring such sectarian deviations.

China: A Zero-Tolerance Policy:

China enforces some of the strictest laws against what it labels as **"heterodox teachings"**, a term broadly used for cults or so-called evil religions. In 1999, the government passed legislation to ban groups considered to be "**disruptive to social order**," with severe penalties for those promoting superstitions or deifying leaders. The crackdown on the Falun Gong movement marked a defining moment in this policy's application. While the Chinese model has faced international condemnation for human rights violations, it reflects a governance model that prioritizes state control and societal conformity over religious pluralism.

United States: Freedom with Accountability:

In the United States, the First Amendment guarantees religious freedom, making it difficult to outlaw any group purely based on belief systems. However, the U.S. legal system actively prosecutes crimes like abuse, fraud, unlawful imprisonment, or psychological manipulation if committed within a religious or spiritual context. Rather than banning groups outright, American law holds individuals accountable for specific criminal acts, offering a more decentralized but constitutionally grounded approach to cult-related offenses.

Germany: Monitoring with Caution:

Germany's federal system allows for close observation of groups suspected of threatening democratic principles. Through the *Federal Office for the Protection of the Constitution*, certain religious or ideological organizations are monitored, especially if their teachings incite social division or violate basic human rights. Germany's vigilance is informed by its historical experiences, although this cautious scrutiny occasionally invites criticism for potentially overstepping boundaries of religious liberty.

Belgium: Information and Awareness:

Belgium adopted a more observational approach. In 1998, a parliamentary commission published a list of 189 organizations identified as potentially harmful sects. This led to the formation of the *Centre for Information and Advice on Harmful Sectarian Organizations*, which focuses on research, education, and public awareness. Rather than immediate legal action,

Belgium emphasizes empowering citizens and professionals to recognize signs of sectarian influence.

Japan: A Turning Point After Tragedy:

Japan's legal response emerged starkly after the 1995 sarin gas attack in Tokyo by Aum Shinrikyo, a doomsday cult. In response, the Japanese government implemented laws allowing authorities to surveil and restrict dangerous organizations. The ***Subversive Activities Prevention Act*** and the ***Organization Control Law*** provide legal mechanisms for dissolving groups engaged in acts of terrorism or illegal confinement. These laws reflect a national resolve to never repeat the horrors inflicted by Aum Shinrikyo's violent ideology.

While these laws have faced criticism from some human rights and religious freedom advocates, who argue they may overreach or unfairly target minority faiths, they also serve as necessary tools to protect vulnerable individuals from manipulation, coercion, and psychological harm. The challenge lies in drawing the line between freedom of belief and protection from abuse.

In our country, we demand:

- A national agency to monitor, report, and act on cult-related activities (like MIVILUDES in France).
- Laws that recognize **psychological manipulation and spiritual coercion** as a form of **abuse**, especially against minors.
- Legal mechanisms to **dissolve harmful organizations** that operate under the guise of spirituality but are destroying families.
- Sensitization of police, judiciary, and media so they understand the **covert tactics** used by such groups.

This is not a matter of religion. It is a matter of **mental autonomy, human dignity,** and **parental rights.**

I urge you to act; not when another tragedy unfolds, but now, before more families are broken.

*****

A Call to Awareness and Action:

If this story resonates with you or stirs a desire to uncover the truth, I invite you to reach out. The reality of this **AIVV, Amol,** and the evidence I have gathered deserve to be known, not just for my daughter's sake, but for the countless others who might be at risk of falling prey to such manipulation.

To access the details of my case and the documented evidence I have painstakingly collected, please contact me through email, **sanmatrika@gmail.com**. Your interest and support mean more than I can express.

Together, we can shine a light on the shadows these exploitative cults thrive. Together, we can create awareness, spark meaningful conversations, and protect others from enduring the pain and loss that so many families, including mine, have experienced.

Your voice, your support, and your commitment to spreading awareness could be the difference that saves someone's child, sibling, or friend. Let's join hands to ensure that no one else falls victim to the deceptive allure of such organizations.

****

CHAPTER XII

A Story Unfinished: A Promise for the Future

The story is not over; it is just waiting for the right moment to turn the page.

This book is not the conclusion of my story; it is merely the first part. My fight to save my daughter, to bring her back from the grasp of manipulation and control, is far from over. The battle continues, and my unwavering dedication remains as strong as ever.

Each day, I hold on to the hope that one day, I will once again embrace my daughter, free from the chains that bind her, free to be the beautiful, compassionate soul she always was. I dream of the day when her smile will no longer be burdened by fear and coercion, when her laughter will once again echo with the freedom of her spirit.

When that day comes, this story will have a second part: a tale of redemption, healing, and the triumph of love over darkness. It will not just be my story anymore; it will be hers as well. Together, we will share the journey from both sides: the pain and resilience of a mother and her struggles and awakening of a daughter.

Through her voice, the world will come to understand the depths of manipulation she endured, the courage it took to break free, and the strength she found within herself. It will be a story of truth, of breaking chains, and of shining a light into the dark corners where deceit and exploitation hide.

Until that day, this book is my promise to my dearest Laaddo and every family fighting a similar battle: **I will not stop, and I will not give up.**

The love between a mother and her child is unbreakable, and no force on this earth can destroy it.

****

A Note to My Precious Daughter

My dearest Laaddo,

If these pages ever find their way to you, know that they reflect the depth of my love for you: a love without bounds, without conditions, and without end. I write these words with trembling hands and a heart that refuses to surrender, because they are meant for you. I understand you may feel misunderstood, and that the path you have chosen may seem beyond my comprehension. But Laaddo, hear this: no matter where life leads you, no matter how distant you may feel, my commitment to you will always remain unwavering, constant, and everlasting.

There are days when the pain of separation threatens to break me, when memories flood in of your tiny hand curled into mine, bedtime stories and whispered dreams, your laughter over the smallest things, and the tears we wiped from each other's eyes. I remember how your voice trembled when you hugged me goodbye and the way you looked at me during our meetings, even as you tried to hide your emotions. I hold onto the moment in the ashram when you reminded me of the girl I once knew, a gesture so small yet so meaningful that it spoke volumes of your love for me, even amid everything.

I am not angry with you, nor do I blame you. You are as much a victim of these circumstances as I am, and I ache for the pain and confusion you must be feeling. But my sweet Laaddo, I also want you to know that you are stronger than you realize, braver than you think, and entirely capable of breaking free from anything that binds you. I have never stopped believing in you. I know the kind, thoughtful, and loving daughter who once stood by my side is still there beneath the layers of confusion and influence.

*Every single day, I pray for the moment when I can hold you close again, without fear or barriers. I dream of the day when we can laugh together, share stories, and heal the wounds this journey has inflicted on both of us. **I know you will return to me**, and when you do, my arms will be open, ready to welcome you home. Until that day, I will keep fighting, not just for you but with you in my heart.*

*You are never alone. No matter what has happened or what you think I might feel, you are my daughter, my pride, and my heart, **and in this world, you are my world.***

With all my love,
Maa

100

****

About The Author

Sanmaatrika is a pen name chosen with deep intention. It means a mother devoted to truth, healing, and the sacred bond between mother and child. This name reflects the spiritual strength and courage that arose within her after her daughter was quietly pulled into the grip of a spiritual cult. As a pen name, it symbolizes her journey from being a dedicated mathematics teacher and quiet nurturer to becoming a fearless voice speaking out for love, truth, and protection against manipulation.

With over five years of experience as a teacher, Sanmaatrika built a life centered on education, values, and care. Her classroom was a place of learning, structure, and inspiration. However, nothing could prepare her for the emotional storm that began when her only daughter, brought up with love and purpose, suddenly walked into a world filled with secrecy and control. A journey of pain, discovery, and deep inner transformation followed.

This book is her debut work, a reflection of real-life events that shook her to the core and yet brought out the deepest strength within her. It is not just a story of loss, but a declaration of love, resilience, and divine support. From sleepless nights to courtroom visits, from silent tears to miraculous signs from the universe, every page carries the echo of a mother's heart that refused to give up.

She writes not for sympathy but to awaken minds and hearts. She writes to ensure that no other family has to suffer in silence. Her mission is rooted in truth, fueled by love, and guided by grace. This book is the first step in a larger journey to reclaim not just her daughter, but every child caught in the trap of blind belief.

Sanmaatrika believes that the story is not over yet. This is only Part One. Part Two will be written when her daughter returns, and when healing finds its full circle.

Epilogue: The Vigil

Epilogue: The Vigil

Every picture on the wall is a fragment of my heart; a glimpse of the daughter I raised with dreams, love, and unwavering hope.

In the quiet of the night, when the world retreats into sleep, I close my eyes, and the hum of memory swells: the warm morning hugs, her triumphant dance after taking the first steps, the bedtime stories punctuated by yawns and giggles. I see her bright face lifting toward me, hear her small voice calling, "Maa!" across every room we ever shared.

A gentle resolve settles over my grief. Though silence presses in from every side, my spirit speaks volumes: love endures beyond locked doors; hope endures beyond silent nights.

In this still hour, I sit alone on the floor, I remain vigilant, wrapped not in luxury but in memories, each one a lantern against the dark. And as the world sleeps on, my heart stays awake, holding Laaddo's paper promise close, waiting for the dawn that will bring her home.

This is where Part One of our story rests. The pages fall silent, but a mother's love never does. This is merely an interlude, the silence between two heartbeats. Her absence does not dim the flame; it waits, alive, for her return. The next chapter awaits...

To be continued....